7

BIRDS AND BEASTS

Animal songs, games and activities

Chosen by Sheena Roberts
Drawings by David Price
Teaching notes by Gill Standring

A & C Black · London

First published 1987 by
A & C Black (Publishers) Ltd
35 Bedford Row, London WC1R 4JH
© 1987 A & C Black (Publishers) Ltd

Printed in Great Britain by Hollen Street Press Ltd, Slough, Berkshire.

Cover illustration by Martin Ursell

Inside illustrations by David Price

Zoological adviser Gill Standring (Assistant Education Officer at London Zoo)

Teaching notes and activities by Gill Standring, Sheena Roberts and Veronica Clark.

Accompaniment ideas by Veronica Clark and Sheena Roberts.

Piano accompaniments and second parts (with the exception of the piano accompaniments on pages 54 and 62 by David Moses, and on page 70 by Christopher Norton) by Sheena Roberts and Timothy Roberts.

Edited by Sheena Roberts

2

Contents

Appearance

Habitat

Moving along

Which animal?

Elizabeth Hogg

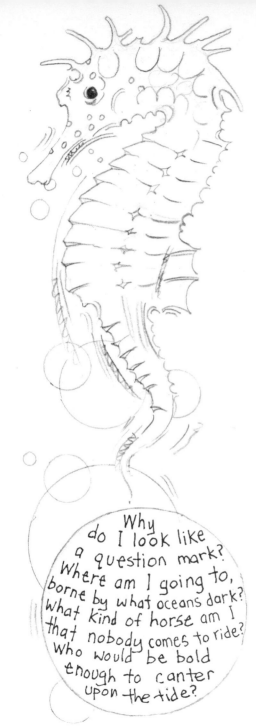

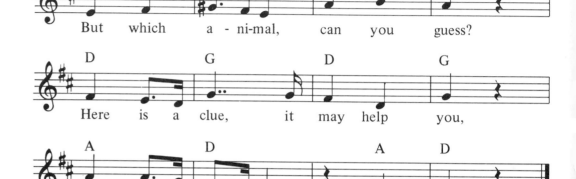

Chorus

I am an animal, oh yes!
But which animal, can you guess?
Here is a clue, it may help you,
I am an animal, oh yes!

Riddle

I am small, I curl up in a ball,
I'm covered in prickles and spikes,
Sharp little nose and beady eyes –
Who am I?

Answer

You're a hedgehog, you're a
  hedgehog,
Yes, you're a hedgehog!

More riddles (answers on p. 78):

Back legs strong for leaping along,
Front legs small and weak,
Pouch for my young and a thick long
  tail –
Who am I?

I have fur that's white as snow,
Powerful jaws and claws,
A big black nose, enormous paws –
Who am I?

Size of a rat, but prettier than
  that,
I have a bushy tail,
Twinkling eyes and a coat of grey –
Who am I?

I'm black and white and I stand
  upright,
I have wings but I can't fly,
Sleek, oily feathers, and a strong,
  sharp beak –
Who am I?

Why do I look like a question mark? Where am I going to, borne by what oceans dark? What kind of horse am I that nobody comes to ride? Who would be bold enough to canter upon the tide?

This is a riddling game song with a simple structure for making up new riddles.

Divide into two groups, or soloist and group (A and B). Everyone sings the chorus, then Group A sings the riddle and Group B sings the answer. Should Group B get stuck, Group A can –
– mime the answer
– allow them to ask questions with yes/no answers about habitat, homes, diet, defences and so on.

Before making up your own riddles, which must refer as clearly as possible to just one animal, it will help to discuss classifications – fish, birds, mammals, insects etc, as well as more detailed aspects of appearance such as coverings, size, face shape etc (see opposite).

Variations – restrict the choice of animals to those you have been studying, e.g.

I am a predator . . .
I am a butterfly . . .

Activities

Riddle pictures – one person thinks of an animal then describes its appearance to the others, who have to draw a picture of it – then guess what the animal is. (Or, one person describes a fabulous creature for the others to draw: 'I was down in the swamp the other day, and I saw . . .' Compare results. Is this the origin of mythical beasts?)

Who am I? – a card with the name of a different animal is attached to the back of each person, so that *they* can't see who they are but everyone else can. Each person has to discover their own identity by asking the others questions with yes/no answers about themselves.

Animal whispers

Accompaniment ideas
When the song is very familiar, try:
Chorus
Tambour – tap lightly with hand

Two-toned woodblock

Tambourine – tap once per word on 'Oh yes' and 'Can you guess?'

Triangle – one tap on 'clue'.

Riddle and Answer
Tambourine – shaken then tapped

Identification
These are some aspects of appearance to think about when making up riddles:

Coverings – hair, fur, skin, feathers, scales, wool, shell, spines. (Also quality of covering – rough, smooth, sleek, shiny, fluffy; and quantity – thickness and length of hair ...)

Overall size and shape – rounded or angular, narrow and long or short and stocky ...

Head shape and features – nose: long/short, large/small; ears: pointed/rounded, erect/drooping ... eyes: how many?, facing forwards/to the sides/all round, inset/protruding, round/oval/almond ... whiskers, horns, antlers, teeth; eyelids and lashes ...

Tail – long, short, stiff, prehensile, tufted ...

Feet – nails, claws, hooves, pads, thumb and fingers, 1/2/3/4/5 toes per foot, same or different fore and hind ...

Locomotion – wings, webbed feet, fins, sharp claws, strong hind legs, light feet and long legs ...

Colouring – single/multi-coloured; colour patterns – stripes, spots, bands, regular/irregular ... distinctive position of colour, e.g. robin's red breast ...

A good naturalist's handbook (see the bibliography) will give information on broad classifications within the animal kingdom.

Spotty song

Accompaniment ideas

Spots – think about the kinds of sounds which best describe leopard spots – would they be long or short, rhythmic or random, sparsely or densely grouped? What instrumental, body or vocal sounds would the children choose to make them? Try devising an accompaniment from your ideas. (Introduce the word *staccato*.)

Stripes – think about the sounds which might describe tiger stripes. For example, you might play long thin sounds on a recorder or violin.

Introduction and link – try playing the first four bars of the melody on xylophone, or piano, starting without a break on the last word of the verse. The children could whisper 'spots spots spots spots'.

Variations—How many animals with spotted coverings can the children list? What other distinctive patterns do animals wear on their coats and what are their functions? (Camouflage for both predator and prey, defensive warning signals, attracting a mate etc.) Use your findings to make up new words for lines five and six, e.g.

**Macaws are all colours
Like rainforest flowers**

**Aphids are green,
On a leaf they're not seen**

**A robin's red breast
Says, 'Look, I'm the best!'**

Extend your ideas to include types of covering – hair, scales, feathers, skin, spikes ... What functions do these serve? Make up more verses along these lines:

**A pussycat's fur
Is as warm as his purr**

**A hedgehog is bristly
And spikey and thistly**

Spots, spots, spots, spots,
Spots, spots, spots, spots,
A leopard has lots of spots,
What a lot of spots he's got!
  A tiger has stripes
  Like a whole lot of pipes,
But a leopard has lots of spots.

Not too fast

Spots, spots, spots, spots, Spots, spots, spots, spots, A leo-pard has lots of spots, What a lot of spots he's got! A ti-ger has stripes Like a whole lot of pipes, But a leo-pard has lots of spots.

Cynthia Raza

Activities

Make a frieze of animal coverings. Use a wide range of techniques to convey a variety of textures and markings. Print with potato cuts, fingertips and corks (for spots), and strips of stiff card (for stripes). Take rubbings from bark and other textured surfaces to get peppered, mottled and brindled effects. Use stencils for very bold clearcut markings. Try collage for particular textures, e.g. shiny papers for very sleek coats, fur fabric and materials for fluffier, rougher ones.

Rondo zoo

This is a score for an instrumental improvisation. In the score you can see elephant feet, octopus tentacles, a coiling snake with patterned skin, and hedgehog spikes. Look at the appearance of them all closely – note the sharp points of the hedgehog spikes, the pattern on the snake's skin and so on. What sounds do they conjure up in the children's minds? Talk about the way each animal moves, and where it lives – do more sounds come to mind?

Preparation

After general discussion, divide into groups – one for each animal – and decide in more detail how each group is going to play its part of the score. Here are some ideas:

Elephant feet (great weight, slow movement, wrinkled skin, soft forest floor, or the dry grasses of the savannah) – large drums, tambours, bass pan, bass strings of guitar or cello, bass chords on piano, large cardboard box beaten with a soft mallet, corrugated paper scraped with fingernails ...

Octopus tentacles (flowing, fast, ravelling movements, round suckers, bubbly, watery sounds) – a soft beater run over the bars of a xylophone or glockenspiel, a balloon rubbed between the hands to make it squeak, upturned plastic beakers dropped onto the surface of some water, a slip of paper waved to and fro over the sound hole of a chime bar after striking, water blown through a straw, flowing, undulating sounds on wind instruments ...

Snake (long, continuous movements, zig zag patterns on dry, scaly skin, long coiling body, rainforest sounds) – sand trickler (see page 23), cabassa, sustained bowed notes on cello, zig zag patterns on violin (run fingertip up and down a string while bowing it), scrapers, bird calls on recorder ...

Hedgehog (sharp, short spikey sounds, scuffling movements, leafy undergrowth) – claves, woodblock, bowed staccato notes on violin, soprano xylophone with small wooden beaters (damp each note quickly with the fingers after striking), an inflated paper bag rustled between the hands or tapped with a wooden beater, a real leafy branch rustled ...

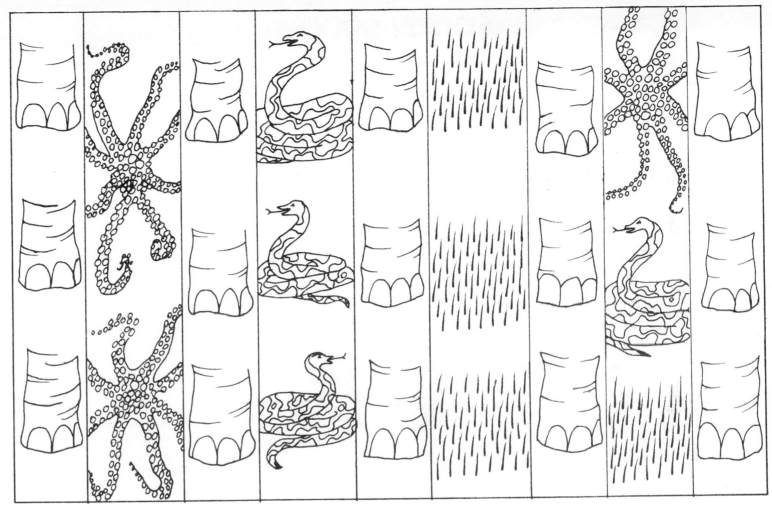

When all the groups have chosen their sounds and how they are going to construct their section, put the whole improvisation together. Use the score here or make a bigger one (each group could provide their own section) that can be displayed along a wall. Read the score from left to right in the usual way, but make your own decisions about the duration, dynamics and organisation of each section. Decide how to link the sections – should there be an abrupt break, or a gradual changeover? Note that the section before last has octopus, snake and hedgehog – should the groups play together or in turn?

Question: a rondo is a piece of music in which one element keeps coming back. Which section is the rondo in *Rondo Zoo*?

More Rondo Zoos

When they have finished playing this *Rondo Zoo*, the children might try making up another based on different animals. Suggest that they look carefully at real animals or pictures in books before drawing their score. Which element will be their rondo?

Abstract skin scores

Select a number of photographs or drawings of patterns on animal coats – leopard spots, zebra stripes, a multi-coloured butterfly wing, a tortoise shell. Ask one person to choose one or more instruments from a broad range, and then to 'play' the pattern of a coat of their choice. What they play should simply be what the pattern itself suggests, e.g. a wide band of colour tapering to a point might suggest a loud, broad, sustained sound fading out to a thin quiet sound. This could be created by rubbing a soft beater to and fro over several bars of a glockenspiel and gradually narrowing the sweep of the beater down to two bars then one. This can be used as an activity for the sounds corner.

Peter Stacey and Biddy Wells

Hi! said the elephant

Hi! said the elephant, look at me,
I've got a long trunk, can you see?
It's an arm, it's a leg, it's a hand, it's a nose:
It pulls and it pushes, and it sucks and it blows.
Have you ever seen a long trunk quite so fine?
Would you like to have a long trunk – like mine?

Hi! said the pussycat, look at me,
I've got whiskers, can you see?
Long, spiky hairs sticking out from my face:
They help me to feel if I can squeeze through a space.
Have you ever seen whiskers quite so fine?
Would you like to have whiskers – like mine?

Hi! said the leopard, look and see,
I've got spots but you can't spot me.
In my camouflage coat in a forest I might
Be a leaf or a shadow or a trick of the light.
Have you ever seen a spotted coat quite so fine?
Would you like to have a spotted coat – like mine?

Hi! said the rabbit, look at me,
I've a fluffy white tail, can you see?
When I wobble my behind and it flashes up and down,
It's a signal to the other rabbits danger is around.
Have you ever seen a fluffy white tail so fine?
Would you like a fluffy white tail – like mine?

Hi! said the tortoise, look at me,
I've got a hard shell, can you see?
It's a nice suit of armour and wherever I may roam
I am safe from attack and I'm always at home.
Have you ever seen a hard shell quite so fine?
Would you like to have a hard shell – like mine?

Bright and fast

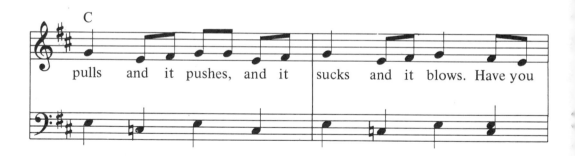

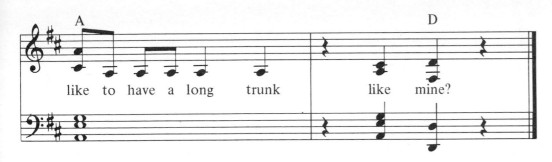

like to have a long   trunk   like   mine?

Sandra Kerr

Accompaniment ideas

Pitched percussion – play one stroke for each letter on the first and third beats of each bar i.e.

D   D   C   C

Hi, said the *el*ephant *look* at *me*

(In the last bar play on the second and third beats – on 'like mine.')

D D	C C	D D	D D
D D	D D	C C	C C
D D	D G	A A	– A D	

Discuss the kinds of sounds appropriate to each animal – their quality, pitch, duration. Having chosen what instruments to use (or vocal or body sounds), think about how they can be used as an accompaniment. For example, you might use some of the rhythm patterns from the melody. Here are some ideas:

Elephant – upturned cardboard box slapped with alternate hands

loudly

Cat – wire brush on cymbal

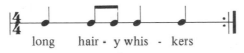

long   hair - y whis - kers

Leopard – tubular woodblock struck on alternate sides

Rabbit – tambour and soft stick

white   fluf-fy tail   bob-bing
softly

Tortoise – scraper

hard _____ shell

Link – between the verses play the next animal's sound very softly as if in the distance. Make the sound get louder as the animal approaches, finishing the crescendo on 'Hi!'

Activities

Why does a giraffe have a long neck? And why is a mole covered in smooth, velvety fur? Choose an animal like a giraffe, and investigate the functions of its appearance. You might examine its habitat, diet, defences and so on. How do these factors affect things like size, basic shape, covering and distinctive features. Investigate other animals in the same way and use the findings to make up new verses for the song. Concentrate, as the song does, on one feature at a time.

A giraffe's long legs and very long neck help it to feed on foliage too high for other animals to reach and give it a grandstand view of approaching predators.

The smooth, velvety fur of the mole enables it to go backwards and forwards in its tunnel without turning round.

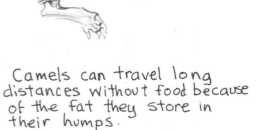

Camels can travel long distances without food because of the fat they store in their humps.

Chicks grow into chickens

Chicks grow into chickens,
Calves grow into cows,
Sycamore seeds grow into trees,
But cubs grow into lions and tigers,
Badgers, foxes, leopards and wolves, and bears.

Foals grow into horses,
Kittens grow into cats,
Fresh green shoots sprout out of roots,
But cubs grow into lions and tigers,
Badgers, foxes, leopards and wolves, and bears.

Pups grow into seals or dogs,
Lambs grow into sheep,
Bulbs can grow into daffodils,
But cubs grow into lions and tigers,
Badgers, foxes, leopards and wolves, and bears.

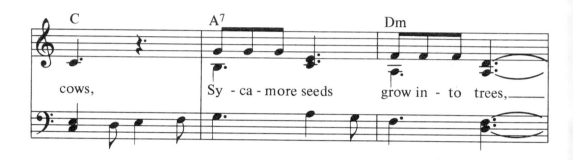

Old friends

Our old dog has a face like a frog,
Eats a lot, sleeps a lot, our old dog.
Our old cat is far too fat,
Sits where I want to sit, our old cat.
Our young pup chews everything up,
Chases the tennis ball, our young pup.
Our young kitty is scratchy and spitty,
Hunts yellow butterflies, our young kitty.
The young ones play with us out in the street,
Their whiskery faces are furry and sweet.
But old dog and old cat are loving and kind.
Whatever we say to them,
they don't mind.

Elizabeth Hogg

Accompaniment ideas
Pitched percussion – play one stroke for each letter on the first and second main beats of the bar:

| C | | C | G | — |
Chicks grow into chickens,

| G | | G | C | — |
Calves grow into cows,

| E | E | D | | D | A |
Sycamore seeds grow into trees,

| G | G | | C | C |
But cubs grow into lions and tigers,

| C | C | C | | B |
Badgers, foxes, leopards and wolves, and

| C ||
bears.

For fun, indicate young and old by alternating high and low-pitched instruments, e.g. soprano glockenspiel and bass xylophone. The notes in **bold** are played by the bass instrument.

Claves

ba - by bear

Bass tambour

bars 1-7   bars 8-12

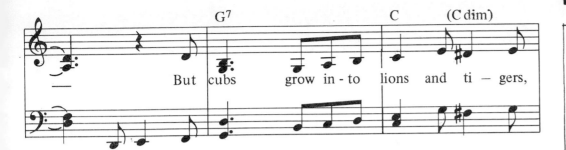

But cubs grow in-to lions and ti—gers,

Bad-gers, fox-es, leo-pards and wolves, and bears.

David Moses

Here are some more names of young animals. Find out what they grow into so that you can make up new verses to the song. (Answers on page 78.)

Kid, fawn, kit, whelp, gosling, cygnet, squab, eyas, larva, tadpole, caterpillar

Cub is the name for the young of many different animals, and so is calf. Try and find out which, and then change the second half of the song to:

But calves grow into cows and ...

Activities

Draw a picture of a young animal and its parent and then describe the differences in their appearance. Note things like *shape* – rounded/angular; *size* – small/large; *texture of covering* – fluffy/rough; *eyes* – large/relatively smaller; *colour* – spotty/one colour; *legs* – long/relatively short; *head* – large/relatively smaller, and so on.

How old is old? The lifespan of a butterfly may be as short as two weeks, whereas a tortoise may live to be a hundred years old. Make a chart of the lifespan of a number of different animals, and see if you can think of any reasons why they may live a very short life or a very long one.

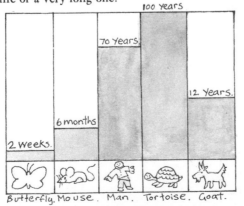

Butterfly. Mouse. Man. Tortoise. Goat.

Elephants and camels

Everyone stands in a ring with one person chosen to be leader. The leader stands in the centre, points to one person and says: Elephant.

The person pointed to bends at the waist, clasps hands and swings them from side to side like a trunk. The two people on either side make elephant ear shapes with their arms all this has to happen:– At the same time!

When the leader says camel, the elephant trunk changes into a hump, and the ears change to a head and tail – all at the same time. The leader points to someone else and says elephant and so on.

Variation: earwig. All three stand with legs apart and bent at the knee one behind the other. The first person holds up his arms like antennae; the third person holds arms hooked like the forceps.

If anyone makes a mistake or hesitates, then the centre person of the threesome goes to the middle of the ring and joins in pointing to the others. With very small children, play making one animal at a time before going on to two. Build up a repertoire of animal shapes to make.

11

Free to roam

On the *first day* of my holiday
My mum said, what will you do today?
So I thought and I said, I'll go to the zoo,
Yes, that's what I'll do, I'll go to the zoo,
Cos I think I might meet a *tiger* or two,
Yes, that's what I'll do, and that's what I'll do,
I'll go and meet a *tiger* or two – in the zoo.

So I did and I went to the tiger house,
And I watched and waited quiet as a mouse,
And the *tiger* yawned and stared at me,
And stared at me so mournfully.
So I said to the tiger, if you were free,
If we found the key, if we set you free,
What would you do? Where would you be?
Where would you be if you weren't – in the zoo?

Verse

If I were a tiger free to roam,
I'd hunt my prey in my forest home,
Where the grass grows thick and the trees grow tall,
And the burning sun makes the shadows fall.
You won't see me spring, you won't hear me run
For I am the colour of shadow and sun.

Chorus – substitute *second day* for *first day*, *condor*
for *tiger*, and *glared and stared* for *yawned and stared*

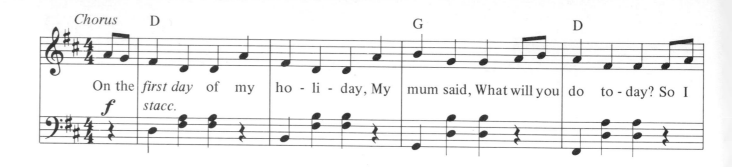

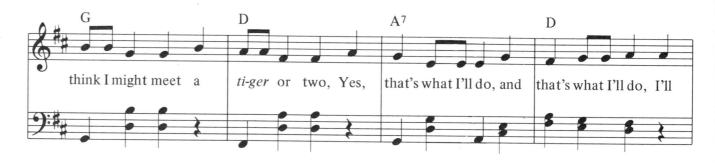

Free to roam

Verses 2-4

Verse

If I were a condor free to roam,
I'd fly to my Andes mountain home,
To my nest in the rocks on the mountainside,
Then high in the sky I'd soar and glide,
Till I spied a dead sheep far below
And with claws at the ready, it's down I'd go.

Chorus – substitute *third day*, *polar bear*, and
stretched and stared

Verse

If I were a polar bear free to roam
On the floating ice I call my home,
Where the trees don't grow and the north winds blow
And the world is white with ice and snow,
I'd dive for fish in the icy storm
With my snow white coat to keep me warm.

Chorus – substitute *fourth day*, *camel*, and
chewed and stared

If I were a camel free to roam
In the desert sands I'd be at home,
There I'd speed along on my padded feet
And go for days before I'd eat.
The hump on my back is my food supply
When there's nothing but sun and sand and sky.

Leon Rosselson

14

Accompaniment ideas

Look at the words and melody of the tiger verse. What do they convey about the tiger's habitat? What instrumental sounds might the children choose to describe burning sun and dark shadow? What sounds would the thick grasses make as the tiger slid by. What other animals might they hear? (Birds, crickets, monkeys.) How do they think this habitat might contrast with that of the child visiting the zoo? What sounds are we accustomed to hearing in our habitat? (Machines, cars, bells, footsteps on pavements, aeroplanes, radios, kitchen sounds, telephones.) Clocks regulate our lives. What regulates animals' lives?

Think about how some of these ideas can be used in an accompaniment. For instance, the chorus might have a very regular, bright pattern on glockenspiel, with two-toned woodblock keeping steady time like a clock ticking (see music example). Whereas in the verse, the sustained bass chords in the piano accompaniment might be played on bass xylophone or cellos, with bright flashes of light breaking through on the highest register of the piano (random clusters of notes), or cymbal (random taps with a hard beater).

How do the other habitats in the song compare with the tiger's? Which would be the quietest? Compare the day-time clamour of a tropical forest with the still heat of a desert day – what happens to them both at night? Which would be the hottest, dryest, highest habitat? Which would support the most complex ecosystem? Decide how to accompany these verses. Here are some ideas:

Condor
Violins – sustain the notes D and A, or harmonics of D and A for a particularly eerie, high-altitude effect.
Wine glasses – run dampened fingers round the rims (you can tune them roughly to D and A by pouring in varying amounts of water).

Polar bear
Piano – random clusters in a high register.
Bottles – blow over the tops (tune them to D and A by filling with water).
Bell spray and triangle – random playing – shivering and flashing.

Camel
Sand trickler – see page 19
Glockenspiel – D and A sustained.
Tambour or drum – plodding crotchet rhythm played with the hands or a soft beater.

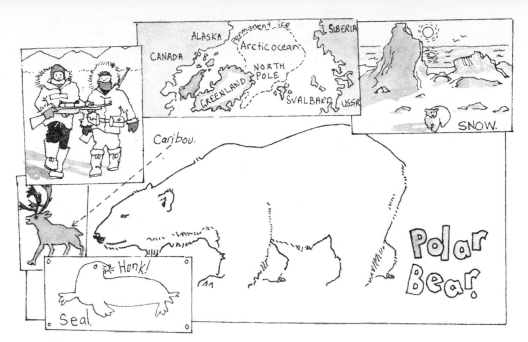

Chorus:

Glockenspiel

(Change to bars of D, G or A where the guitar chord changes)

OR

Claves or two-toned woodblock

OR

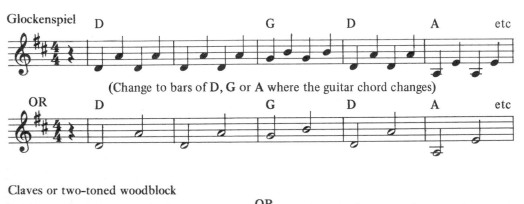

Activities

A habitat is simply a place to live in. An animal's habitat includes soil, air, water, temperature, weather conditions, plants, and other animals – together they form one interdependent *ecosystem*.

How many habitats? Here are some examples – Arctic ice, African grassland, European woodland, a freshwater pond, the ocean. List as many more as the children can think of, then add to them with the aid of a reference book.

Habitat display – choose one of the animals in the song and find out as much as you can about how it depends on its habitat for survival. Where is the habitat found, what other animals and plants does it support, how are they dependent on each other, and what problems do they have to contend with, e.g. very high temperatures, sparse food supplies, human interference and so on. Make a display demonstrating your chosen animal's place in this ecosystem. Make the centrepiece of your display a photograph or drawing of the animal, and surround it with photographs or drawings of the habitat itself, the animal's home, its food and its predators.

You might also include the kind of annotations suggested on page 25. See also page 44 (food chains) and page 65 (food webs).

You might follow this with a display of a more familiar animal and a local habitat, e.g. wood mouse and European woodland. Try making up a wood mouse verse for the song.

Collage – make a collage background on which to mount your habitat display, or make a series of collage pictures showing the different habitats in the song. Here are some ideas:

Tiger – green and brown fabrics and papers for dense foliage and trees, black netting for shadows, rope for creepers.

Condor – blue and grey netting for sky, rough fabrics for rocks, twigs for dead trees.

Polar bear – icy blue shiney papers and fabrics, silver foil and fabric, polystyrene chips, white plastic cloth, lace.

Camel – sand sprinkled over glue on background of yellows and reds, sand paper, scrumpled brown paper for rocks, yellow netting, strips of silver foil for distant mirage.

Says the bee

Come with me, says the bee,
Into the daffodil.
All our house has yellow walls
And honey on the sill.

Come with me, says the bee,
Into the open rose.
Perfume curtains all around,
And pollen on your toes.

Come with me, says the bee,
Into the lily flower.
Sun in your window every sunny day,
Umbrella for a shower.

Malvina Reynolds

VOICES OR KAZOOS

Light and airy

Come with me, says the bee, In - to the daf - fo - dil.

Bzzz

All our house has yel- low_walls And ho-ney on the sill.

Bzzz   Bzzz

Lots of worms

Well, there are lots of worms way under the ground,
Lots of worms that I've never found,
I'll bet they're way down there a-diggin' around,
Way under the ground.

I dug the biggest hole I ever did dig,
The biggest hole, it sure was big!
And when I got to the bottom, you know what I found
Way under the ground?

I found a worm to go on a fishing pole
Down at the bottom of that deep, dark hole,
But I left him alone because he liked his home –
Way under the ground.

Well, there are lots of worms way un - der the ground, ___

Earthy but not slow

Lots of worms that I've ne-ver found_ I'll bet they're way down there a-

Accompaniment ideas

It may help the singers' intonation if the outline of the melody can be played lightly on a glockenspiel or piano. (Keep the singing light and precise, like the movements of the bee):

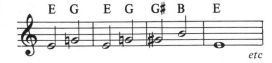

etc

The second part for voices or kazoos is great fun to use if the performers can keep a straight face! Slide up and down between the notes in a long, undulating buzz.

You can create a tinselly buzz in the guitar accompaniment by lacing a strip of tinfoil between the strings at the bridge end. Play a slow strum or arpeggiated finger-pick for maximum buzz.

Make a contrast between bars 1–4 (droney and dark) – cello or guitar, bass E drone – and bars 5–8 (bright, colourful and sweet):

Triangle

Cymbal and soft beater (bars 7–8)

Jingles gently shaken throughout

Voices or glockenspiel

bars 5-8

Activities

A flower and its visitors

Wall display – if possible observe a real flower in its natural setting over a period of days to see who comes to visit. Flowers attract many kinds of insect, centipedes, slugs and snails, which in turn attract predators such as birds and small mammals. To record the findings, collect one of the flowers and press it with its stem and leaves, or make a collage model of it. Mount it on a large sheet of card, and round it display diagrams or pressings of the different parts of the plant, photographs or drawings of its visitors, a note of the visitor's purpose, and what it was that attracted it – scent, nectar, colour, insects etc.

Mobile display – the centrepiece is the flower, made from card, tissue and crêpe paper (the centre of a flower like a daffodil can be made with a yoghurt pot). Make

insects with cork bodies, gauze or net wings, and pipe cleaner legs. Birds may be cut out of card and painted. Some of the visitors can rest on the flower and others can be suspended round it.

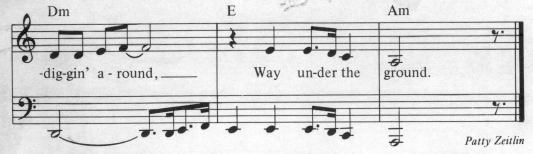

Dm   E   Am

-dig-gin' a - round,_____   Way   un-der the   ground.

Patty Zeitlin

Accompaniment ideas

Earthy bass sounds are needed. The bass line of the piano accompaniment can be plucked on cello or (an approximation) on tea-chest bass. It can also be sung as a second voice part by an adult bass, if it is transposed up an octave – sing *boop-boop-boop-boop* ...

Try this simple part for bass xylophone, guitar (single bass notes - open strings) or

bottles. You need three bottles and three people to blow over the tops of them – tune them to A, E and D by filling them with water to different levels. Play, or blow, one note per bar, or attempt the rhythm of the melody:

| A | A | A | E | A | D | E | A ||

For fun, imagine what sounds earthworms might make under ground as they chomp through dead leaves and push themselves

through holes, then try imitating them, e.g. rub a balloon between the hands, scrumple a plastic eggbox or tap it with a hard beater:

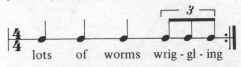

lots   of   worms   wrig - gl - ing

Tape the song on a tape recorder with adjustable speeds – what happens when it is slowed down?

Activities

Make a terrareum (see page 78) so that you can study earthworms as they work away under ground, aerating the soil, and transforming dead leaves into humus.

Dead wood conservation – maximise the micro habitats available to fungi, beetles and other insects by conserving or introducing dead wood into your garden or school grounds. This means allowing broken branches or logs to lie unmoved so that the whole succession of species that live off the wood, or each other, may gradually process the wood back into soil. You can introduce some logs or even just the trimmings of overhanging branches to a shady corner to make an ideal micro habitat which can be observed from time to time as it decays. Birds attracted to dead trees for nesting sites and for insect food include kestrels, nuthatches, owls, wrens, woodpeckers, tree creepers, and the tit family.

Saeynu

Saeynu, saeynu, lamidbar saeynu,
Saeynu, saeynu, lamidbar saeynu,
   Lililili li lili li lili
   Lililili li lili li lili
   Lililili li lili li lili
   Lamidbar saeynu.
Lamidbar saeynu al debeshot g'ma lim
Ve al sefrehem yets al tselu pa'amonim
   g'dolim.
Saeynu, saeynu, lamidbar saeynu,
Saeynu, saeynu, lamidbar saeynu.

Translation

Carry us, carry us to the desert,
Carry us, carry us to the desert.
   Lililili li (camel bells)
   Carry us to the desert.
Carry us to the desert on the
   backs of camels
And the saddles will ring with
   big bells.
Carry us, carry us to the desert ...

Lyrics under the music:

La - mid - bar_____ sa - ey - nu___
al — se-fre — hem yets al tse - lu pa' -

al de-be-shot g'ma lim, Ve —
—am - o — nim g'do — —lim.

Traditional Israeli

Accompaniment ideas

The tuned percussion part calls for two players (part 1 – stems turned down; part 2 – stems turned up). The parts need to be played lightly, particularly part 2 which is on the unaccented beats of the bar.

Tambour tapped with hand

de - sert song

Drum and soft beater – one tap per bar.

Tambourine – tapped in the rhythm of the words of lines 1, 2 and 6, i.e.

(sa - ey-nu ...) *etc*

Bell spray throughout lines 3–5 (lililili)

Sand trickler – tape together three or four cylindrical containers end to end (they need to be about 8–10 cm in diameter). In the centre of each of the inner lids and bases cut a hole about 4 cm in diameter. The lid and base of the end containers are left intact. Pour in a mug of dry sand or rice and seal the lid. Tilt the instrument slowly and listen to the sand trickling through. Use it to give an impression of dry heat, wind-blown dust and sand.

sand trickler.

Natural deserts cover 6% of the Earth's ice-free land surface – the African Sahara being the largest of them. They are positioned on areas of the continents where humid air has lost all moisture on mountains or inland. But another 28% of the Earth's ice-free land is already affected or likely to be affected by desertification – a man-made process. The causes are over-cultivation, deforestation, over-grazing and poor irrigation.

As an area turns to desert, it becomes less able to sustain animal – and human – life. The main problems for survival are
1) temperature control – overheating during the day turning to bitter cold at night,
2) lack of water, 3) lack of food (vegetable and animal), and 4) dust and sand storms.

Adaptations to desert life: small animals like kangaroo rats, hopping mice, gerbils, fennec foxes and pack rats burrow deep down into the earth to nest and store food where the conditions are cooler and more humid. When the desert suddenly flowers in the rain, insects emerge from eggs or pupae which have lain dormant for months during dry periods. Large animals need special physiological mechanisms to conserve water and store food (see camel, pages 9 and 14). Birds find survival particularly difficult, but some species manage – eagles and vultures soar high in the sky where the air is cooler during the day, while smaller birds hide in holes or cracks between rocks. The sand grouse may fly as much as 50 miles to collect water for its chicks – it stands in water letting its feathers soak up the moisture, which the chicks suck off on its return.

Sea dive

Splash into the waves in a shower of droplets,
Past the flying fish skimming o'er the foam.
Leave the sea-birds screaming, wheeling
Round their cliff-top nesting home.

Just below the pale green surface
Cormorants dive with flashing grace.
Seaweed shifting, plankton drifting,
Jellyfish glide at gentle pace.

Down through shoals of darting fishes
Chased by sharks with fearful jaws.
Tuna streaking, dolphins squeaking,
Whales cruise by to far-off shores.

Flatfish, starfish move along the sea-bed,
Crab and lobster sideways crawl.
Worms a-wriggling, eels a-squiggling,
Anemones cling to coral walls.

Dark and still are the waters of the ocean
Far from the winds and the crashing seas.
Deep down under, gaze with wonder,
Sea-green world of mysteries.

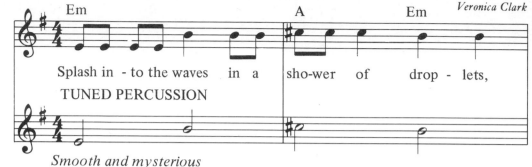

Veronica Clark

Splash in - to the waves in a sho-wer of drop - lets,

TUNED PERCUSSION

Smooth and mysterious

Past the fly-ing fish skimming o'er the foam. Leave the sea - birds

Movement and dance

Practise movement ideas in conjunction with sound effects (those suggested or the children's own), then select from them to devise a dance. Here are some ideas:

Flying fish – a few children at a time, running then taking long, low leaps together.

Sea birds – using arms as wings, swooping, diving, swerving, gliding and bending and stretching on to tiptoe to give the idea of height.

Cormorants – make swift, diving movements with the head leading, and with arms tucked into sides. On breaking through the imaginary water level, slow down, rise and leave the water in a burst of wing flaps.

Jellyfish – crouch in a ball with head, arms and knees tucked into body, then quickly stretch out all limbs, and take a few quick steps backwards. Move in synchronised groups.

Shoals of fish – using arms fluttering at sides as fins, move quickly round the room in a large group, all changing direction together (on a given signal).

Shark – arms held out in front as jaws. One or two children move through the shoal, changing direction at own speed and time, in steady glides.

Whales – vast, slow glide by group of children with hands on each other's backs, heads lowered, taking long, slow paces together and rising and falling on bended knees and tiptoes to give an impression of undulating movement.

Flatfish – gentle waving movements with flat hands, arms spread out to sides and head held on side, walking sideways.

Starfish – spreadeagled limbs and slow sideways movement.

Crabs – on all fours, crawling slowly then making quick sideways rushes.

Diver – descending movements, turning, sinking, settling. Slow, curious examination of environment.

Am · · · Em · · · B⁷ · · · E(m)

scream-ing, wheel-ing | Round their cliff-top | nest-ing home.

(G♯ *last verse*)

Accompaniment ideas

Discuss how you can convey an idea of the different sea levels described in each verse. Compare the noise and turmoil of breaking waves and spray on the surface with the kaleidoscope of broken light and darting shoals of small fish just below; further down are the deep, green waters and the dark forms of larger sea creatures cruising by, and lower still, the dark sea-bed.

Draw out the children's own ideas for sound effects, and help them to experiment widely. Discuss timbre, volume, rhythm (regular or free), pitch and direction of pitch. Use anything available to make sounds – instruments, voices, junk, etc. The children may evolve their own accompaniment, in which case ignore the ideas given below.

Verse 1

Tuned percussion part – use soprano glockenspiel and hard beaters.

Triangle – tapped hard with metal beater on the first beat of each bar.

Line 1: cymbal clash (*ff*) on 'splash'. Tambourine or bell spray shaken through 'shower of droplets'.

Line 2: finger cymbals in random clusters.

Lines 3–4: cymbal and wire brush – steady taps on minim beats. Voices for mewing gulls.

Verse 2

Tuned percussion part – soprano xylophone or metallophone and soft beaters.

Triangle with wooden beater – as above.

Lines 1–2: glockenspiel or high register of piano – random downward glissandi.

Lines 3–4: cymbal – run a wire brush continuously round the rim.

Verse 3

Tuned percussion part – alto xylophone or metallophone and soft beaters.

Small gong or cymbal tapped with soft beater on first beat of each bar.

Line 1: bell spray or tambourine shaken twice on 'darting fishes' *f > f >*

Line 2: wooden clappers tapped together on crotchet beats.

Line 3: soprano glockenspiel – upward glissandi on 'streaking' and 'squeaking'.

Line 4: largest drum, tambour or gong available – four minim beats.

Verse 4

Tuned percussion part – bass xylophone or metallophone and soft beaters.

Bottle (tuned to E with water) – blow over the top with very long, slow breaths.

Lines 1–2 (bars 1–4):

guiro   woodblock

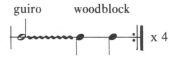 x 4

Lines 3–4: maraccas – shake gently.

Verse 5

Tuned percussion part – omit

Bass xylophone or metallophone or piano – play lowest E on first beat of every bar like a tolling bell.

Bottle – as above (Verse 4)

Line 4: cymbal – soft, shimmering clash on 'mysteries'

Activities

Sea-life mobile – make a large mobile, showing different levels of life in the sea. Cut out the shapes of birds and fish in card, tissue paper, silver foil, and so on. Larger fish can be jointed to give them movement. Cut out the shape then cut it vertically into several pieces. Space them slightly apart then run sticky tape along them horizontally to hold them together. Use upturned margarine tubs with streamers of tissue paper glued round the rim for jellyfish. Use short lengths of cardboard tube threaded onto bent wire, and covered in tissue paper, for eels and worms.

Paint a window with washable powder paints to create a translucent background of changing hues.

The urban hedgehog

There is a hedgehog living near here – he's very shy,
Sometimes we see him, usually at night-time – I wonder why?
If we make the slightest move or any noise at all,
He'll roll up into a very prickly, frightened ball.

He likes eating snails and slugs and – earthworms he finds
Centipedes and spiders and insects – of every kind.
Here he comes a-running, scuttling right up to the door,
Tempted by some scraps of food and a drink of milk he saw.

Sniffing, snuffling, snorting, grunting – his snout can smell
All the dangers in the city – he knows so well.
Dogs and foxes, owls and badgers are his predators,
Railway lines and trains can kill him, so can motor cars.

Then in the winter when it's colder – he makes a nest
Using his body pressing the walls hard – for his long rest.
He likes hedges, logs and ditches, under roots of trees,
Holey, sandy banks to hide in, filled with dry, packed leaves.

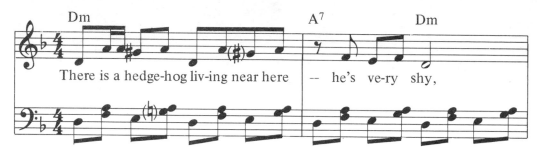

Hedgehog speed

Accompaniment ideas

Think of dry, rustling sounds to use, e.g. scrumpling paper or a plastic eggbox, a tin filled with sand or rice. Here are some ideas:

Tuned percussion – experiment with attaching crinkly paper round the head of the beaters, and play very softly:

'Sandpaper blocks – rub them together to make lovely shuffling sounds. Make pairs of them by pinning or glueing medium grade sandpaper to a couple of small blocks of wood. Pick out some rhythms from the song to play, e.g.

Claves

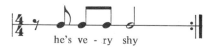

Link – as hedgehogs search at dusk among plants and dead leaves for their diet of slugs, snails and insects, they make a mixture of snorts, snuffles and grunts. Try making up a link, two or four bars long, using voices or instruments to imitate hedgehog sounds.

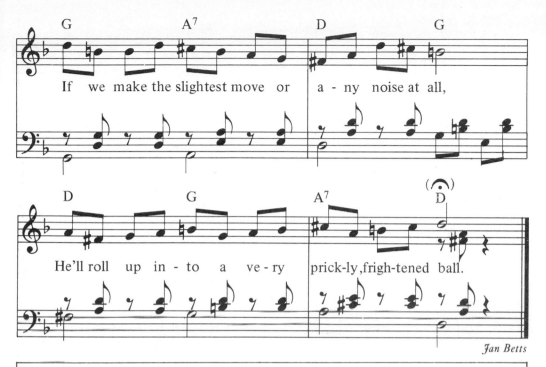

If we make the slightest move or a-ny noise at all,
He'll roll up in-to a ve-ry prick-ly, frigh-tened ball.

Jan Betts

Activities

Discussion – how do animals such as hedgehogs adapt themselves to life in built-up areas? Think of the disadvantages as well as the advantages. Food and shelter may be easier to find, but diseases can spread because of overcrowding. Seasonal changes are less dramatic, but animals become less well-adapted to natural hardships and dangers. While it may be easier to find a mate, battles with neighbours for territory may become more intense. And animals which are very successful at living in towns may come to be regarded by humans as pests if they cause damage or pollution.

Urban habitat survey – survey the surroundings of the school or the children's homes, to find out what kinds of habitat are on offer, and which animals are making use of them. Draw a bird's eye view of the chosen area, showing the position of greenery, hedges, trees, walled secluded areas, wasteland, sheltered spots away from traffic, neglected buildings offering shelter. Observe as thoroughly as possible the animal population, and record sightings on the aerial plan. Draw up a food web (see page 65) showing how the animals and plants depend on each other and on humans for their food supply.

Make a booklet of advice and tips for attracting and sustaining wildlife in the area, school grounds or gardens (see page 78).

Historical habitats – find out what natural habitat was on the site of the children's homes or school before they were built.

Dusk chorus – ask the children to spend ten to fifteen minutes listening for animal sounds at dusk, jotting down a list of those they hear (possibly owls, cats, dogs, swifts, starlings, bats). Try including some of these sounds in the link .

Mamma, lend me your pigeon

Mamma lend me your pigeon to keep comp'ny with mine,
Mamma lend me your pigeon to keep comp'ny with mine.
My pigeon gone wild in the bush, my pigeon gone wild,
My pigeon gone wild in the bush, my pigeon gone wild.

Mamma lend me your penguin to keep comp'ny with mine ...
My penguin gone slide on the ice rink, my penguin gone wild ...

Mamma lend me your reindeer to keep company with mine ...
My reindeer gone ride on the roundabout, my reindeer gone wild ...

Mamma lend me your zebra to keep comp'ny with mine ...
My zebra gone set up a traffic jam, my zebra gone wild ...

Mamma lend me your turtle to keep comp'ny with mine ...
My turtle gone swim in the Thames, my turtle gone wild ...

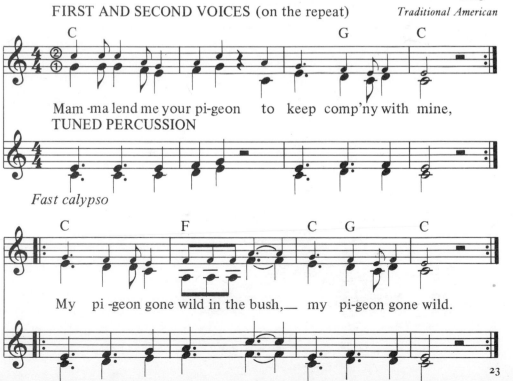

Traditional American

FIRST AND SECOND VOICES (on the repeat)

Mam-ma lend me your pi-geon to keep comp'ny with mine,

TUNED PERCUSSION

Fast calypso

My pi-geon gone wild in the bush,— my pi-geon gone wild.

What can make a hippopotamus smile?

Author unknown

What can make a hippopotamus smile?
What can make him walk for more than a mile?
Not a party with paper hats,
Or cake and candy that can make him fat,
That's not what hippos do.
    They ooze through the gooze without
        any shoes,
    They wade in the water till their lips
        turn blue,
    And that's what makes a hippopotamus
        smile.

What can make a hippopotamus smile?
What can make him walk for more than a mile?
Not a tune on an old violin,
Or listening to the singing wind,
That's not what hippos do.
    They ooze through the gooze ...

What can make a hippopotamus smile?
What can make him walk for more than a mile?
Not a zoom down a slippery slide,
Or going for a bicycle ride,
That's not what hippos do.
    They ooze through the gooze ...

What can make a hippopotamus smile?
What can make him walk for more than a mile?
Not some brand new words to spell,
Or collecting whistles or marbles or shells,
That's not what hippos do.
    They ooze through the gooze ...

What can make a hippopotamus smile?
What can make him walk for more than a mile?
Not a movie or an Irish jig,
Or Halloweening in a funny wig,
That's not what hippos do.
    They ooze through the gooze ...

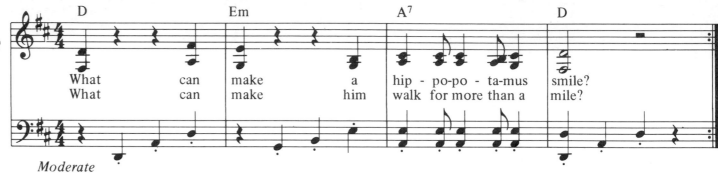

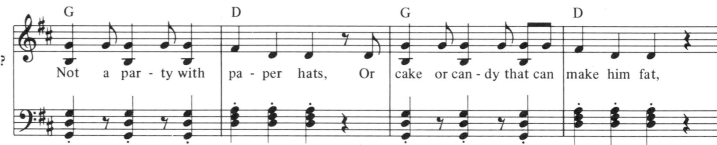

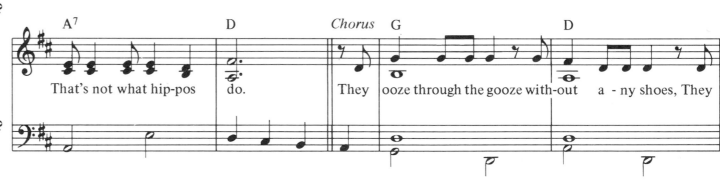

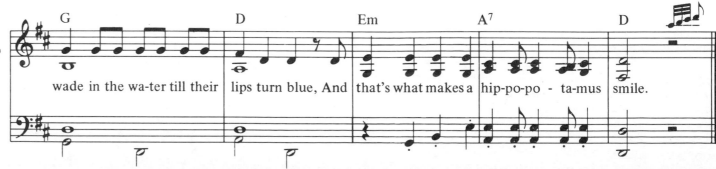

Accompaniment ideas

Try making a contrast between the brightly rhythmic, party atmosphere of the verse, and the sustained oozing of the chorus:

Verse – use light percussion instruments e.g. bars 1-8

Tambourine/maracas/cabassa

Woodblock

bars 9-12

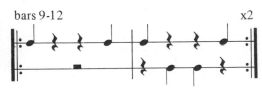

bars 13-14

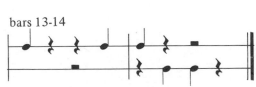

The words give plenty of scope for sound effects – party whizzers, blowing over the tops of bottles (singing wind), a downward glissando on piano (slippery slide), bicycle bell, whistles and rattles (marbles and shells), spooky voice sounds (Halloweening).

Chorus – try creating muddy, oozing squelches with the following – a sink plunger in a bucket of water (or mud!), mouth pops and squelches, a thin sheet of metal or thick card wobbled.

Activities

Verse variations – make up new versions of the song – what would make a penguin smile – an ice slide? or a bat – a damp, dark cave? What makes the children smile?

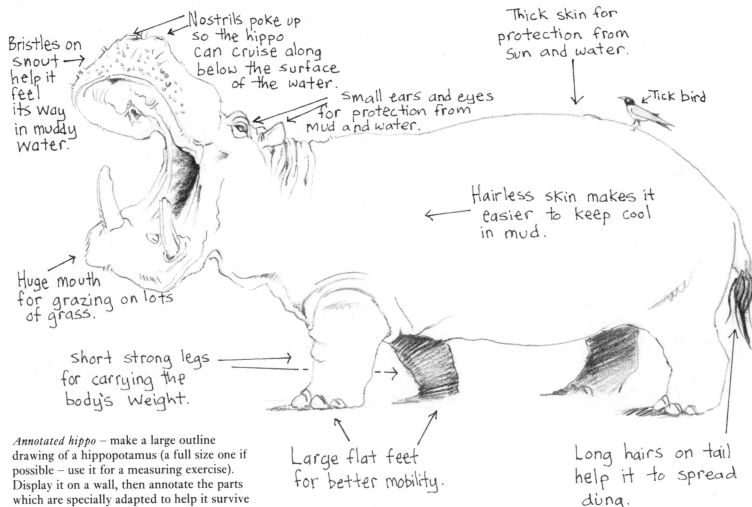

Bristles on snout help it feel its way in muddy water.

Nostrils poke up so the hippo can cruise along below the surface of the water.

Small ears and eyes for protection from mud and water.

Thick skin for protection from sun and water.

Tick bird

Hairless skin makes it easier to keep cool in mud.

Huge mouth for grazing on lots of grass.

Short strong legs for carrying the body's weight.

Large flat feet for better mobility.

Long hairs on tail help it to spread dung.

Annotated hippo – make a large outline drawing of a hippopotamus (a full size one if possible – use it for a measuring exercise). Display it on a wall, then annotate the parts which are specially adapted to help it survive in its habitat. Do the same with other animals, e.g.

Sea-lion – smooth aerodynamic shape for fast underwater swimming, strong, webbed flippers for powerful swimming, fur and blubber for warmth, small ears for conserving heat, large eyes for seeing under water, nostrils which shut tight under water, long stiff whiskers for feeling the way under water.

Polar bear – huge size and thick fur coat for warmth, white coat for camouflaged hunting, large front paws for swimming, flat, spreading paws and furry non-skid soles for gripping on snow and ice, powerful claws, jaws and long neck for reaching out to grab prey, small ears for conserving heat, excellent sense of smell for scenting out prey.

Leopard – strong, springy back legs for pouncing, bendy, springy backbone for vertical leaps in and out of trees, padded feet for stealth, spots for camouflage, long sensitive whiskers for feeling the way in the dark and good eyesight for hunting at dusk, mobile ears and tail for silent signalling.

The hopper

If I could hop as well as a flea,
Gosh, what an athlete I should be!
A flea can hop as high as my knee –
And so, I suppose, it seems to me
I could hop over a largish tree.
Then what astonishing sights
**   I'd see:**
People below, all teeny-wee,
Each with a head the size of a pea!
I'd caper about and shout with glee
That my great big hop had made me
**   free,**
And laugh at everyone: 'Hee-hee-hee,
You never guessed I could hop like
**   a flea!'**

Elizabeth Hogg

Kangaroos like to hop

Kangaroos like to hop,
And zebras like to run,
Horses like to trot,
But I like to lie in the sun.

Panthers like to pounce,
And geese like to fly,
Squirrels like to jump,
But I like to gaze at the sky.

Moderate

Kan-ga-roos like to hop, And
ze-bras like to run,
Hor-ses like to trot, But
I like to lie in the sun.

Leon Rosselson

Activities

Movement poems – talk about how animals move – how many different forms of locomotion are there? (Swimming, flying, running, hopping, wriggling, sliding . . .) Can the children make up a poem of sounds describing movement, e.g.

   Slippery slithery
   Hithery dithery
   Lippety loppety
   Clippety cloppety
   Glide slide . . .

Accompaniment ideas

Choose an instrumental or vocal sound to represent each animal, and play it during the rests in the melody, e.g.

Kangaroo – woodblock or ruler (twanged):

...hop   And

Zebra – tambour tapped with hand:

...run

Horse – coconut shells or yoghurt pots clopped together:

...trot   But

Child – swanee whistle:

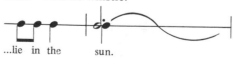

...lie in the   sun.

Try using a guitar or autoharp to give some very light harmonic support – beginner

guitarists will find it easy because of the long gaps between chord changes (play one slow strum per bar). Alternatively, play this sequence on chime bars or other tuned percussion:

| G (G) G | | D (D) D | | |
| C (C) C | | D | | G ||

Activities

Make up new verses – perhaps contrasting fast movers in one verse with slow movers in another, or very noisy movers with very quiet ones, or different techniques of flying.

Follow my leader

Animation

A flea went hopping, hopping, hopping,
Over the field where the grass is green.
On his way he met a grasshopper –
Won't you follow my leader with me?

A grasshopper went hopping, hopping,
Over the field where the grass is green.
On his way he met a little frog –
Won't you follow my leader with me?

A frog went hopping, hopping, hopping,
Over the field where the grass is green.
On his way he met a rabbit –
Won't you follow my leader with me?

A rabbit went hopping, hopping,
  hopping,
Over the field where the grass is green.
On his way we heard him calling –
Won't you follow my leader with me?

A flea went hop – ping, hop – ping, hop – ping,

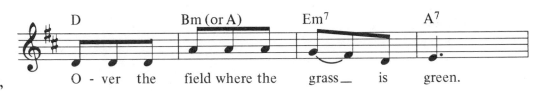
O - ver the field where the grass is green.

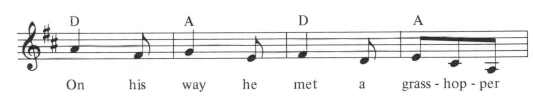
On his way he met a grass - hop - per

Won't you fol - low my lea - der with me?

Jenyth Worsley

Choose a rhythm or sound to represent two different animals. The leader plays one of the sounds e.g. rabbit - woodblock etc, and everyone hops around like a rabbit.

The leader changes to the second sound e.g. snake - maracas shaken continuously and everyone slithers along like snakes. Keep changing the rhythms and think of new ones to add.

A ring game – everyone sits in a circle and one person is chosen to be the flea. When the singing starts, the flea hops off round the outside of the ring. At 'grasshopper', the flea stops, and the nearest person jumps up to be the grasshopper. Both hop off, one behind the other, round the ring. Next time, the frog jumps up, and so on. See if the children can think of enough hopping creatures to add to the song to get everyone up hopping by the end. (Jerboa, kangaroo rat, sandhopper, blackbird . . .)

Variation – change the movement to crawling, creeping, trotting, flying, and so on. Make up a similar sequence of verses with one of these.

Activities

Sets – investigate combinations of locomotion and group them in sets, e.g.

Accompaniment ideas

Tuned percussion – one beat per bar:
Bars 1–12

| D | C# | B | A | :‖ × 3

Bars 13–16

| D | A | A | D ‖

Choose an instrument to characterise each animal and let each join in cumulatively when their verse comes up, e.g.

Flea – triangle, tapped lightly

long   jump

Grasshopper – scraper, scraped and tapped

hop - per   hop - per

Frog – woodblock

frog leap   frog leap

Rabbit – small tambour tapped with fingers

lit - tle hop   lit - tle hop

Birds are flying

Accompaniment ideas
Chorus
Slither box (see page 30), or long shaker, or a rubber beater rubbed lightly over all the bars of a glockenspiel or xylophone.

Verse lines 1–2 (bars 1–4)
Eagle – large guiro or scraper rubbed with a hard beater continuously, then tapped three times:

ea - gle eye

Herring gull – corrugated paper and fingertips – rub lightly and slowly, then three short scrapes on 'greedy eye' as above.

Kestrel – maraca shaken continuously then three short shakes on 'beady eye'.

Kingfisher – triangle tinkled very gently then tapped three times on 'twinkling eye'.

Verse lines 3–4 (bars 5–10)
Glockenspiel glissando (very soft) through line three.
Thin card (two or three sheets held together) flapped through line four.

Activity
Make a flying bird model

garden cane.

wings loosely hinged with wire or string

stiff card

Pull here

Soaring, gliding, swooping, diving,
Birds are flying in the air.
Soaring, gliding, swooping, diving,
Birds are flying while we stand
   and stare.

Have you seen an eagle soaring
   in the sky?
An eagle with its eagle eye.
It swoops right down to the ground
   for its prey,
Grabs the rat and flies away.
   Soaring, gliding . . .

Have you seen a herring gull gliding
   in the sky?
A herring gull with a greedy eye.
It swoops right down to the sea
   for its prey,
Grabs the fish and flies away.
   Soaring, gliding . . .

Have you seen a kestrel hover
   in the sky?
A kestrel with a beady eye.
It swoops right down to the ground
   for its prey,
Grabs the mouse and flies away.
   Soaring, gliding . . .

Have you seen a kingfisher perching
   up on high?
A kingfisher with a twinkling eye.
It dives right down to the river
   for its prey,
Grabs the fish and flies away.

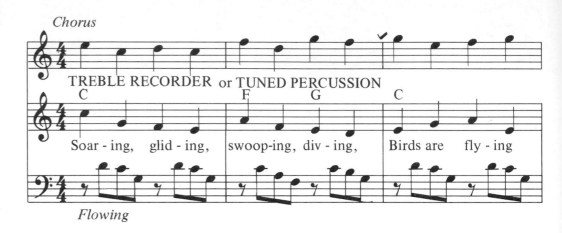

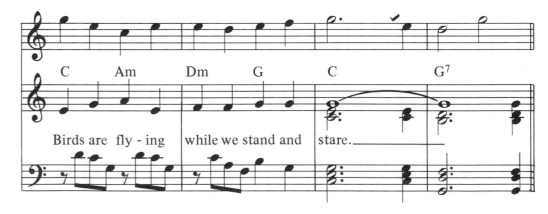

All geese fly

Harriet Powell

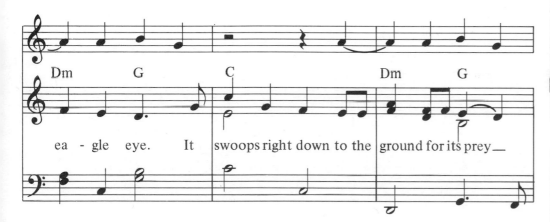

Verse

Have you seen an ea-gle soa-ring in the sky? An ea-gle with its ea-gle eye. It swoops right down to the ground for its prey — Grabs the rat and flies a — way.

One person is the leader and calls out the name of a bird which flies. Everyone else flaps their arms like wings.

The leader goes on changing the animal without pausing between them while the others carry on flapping

Then the leader calls out an animal that doesn't fly. Everyone must stop flapping. Anyone flapping by mistake has to think of three more animals that fly.

The leader can change to another kind of movement. If the leader hesitates, the first person to call out a correct name becomes leader.

Preparation – talk about which birds do and don't fly, which swim and which don't, which hover or dive; then play the game. (Make sets showing the overlaps.)

Activities

Flight – what is necessary for it? *Light weight* (hollow bones in birds, and very thin bones in bats), *flat aerodynamic surface* (wing), *steering*, *good senses*, and *power* (good heart, lungs and muscles).

These qualities are present in three living groups of animals: bats, birds and insects – the only active fliers. Gliders include fish, frogs, snakes, lizards and squirrels.

Magnifying feathers – examine flight feathers and notice how the barbs 'zip' together to form a strong, light surface. Look at contour feathers – those which contribute to the bird's outward form – and the down feathers, which give warmth. Watch how feathers behave when they are thrown into the air.

Human flight – tell the story of *Icarus*, and compare human physique with a bird's. Why is it impossible for humans to fly unaided?

These two songs can be sung separately or in combination. Start with the chorus and first verse of *Who saw the footprints?*, then sing the rabbit verse of *Wild and Wary*, followed by the chorus and rabbit verse of *Who saw the footprints?* Sing the next verse of *Wild Wary*, and so on. Use the link bars in the second song to go from one to the other.

Accompaniment ideas
Use the rabbit, squirrel, hedgehog and fox rhythms for both songs.

Wild and wary bars 1–6 and 11–14, and verses of *Who saw the footprints*:

Rabbit – woodblock or tongue clicks

Squirrel – tapped tambourine or voice

chicka chick…

Deer – xylophone or voices humming, and slither box (tip a long, flat box containing sand from side to side)

mm_ mm_ mm mm

Hedgehog – scraper or voices (short snorts)

Fox – wire brush rubbed round a large cymbal, or voices

ssssh _____

Wild and wary bars 7–10
chime bars   xylophone

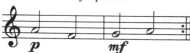
p   *mf*

Animal rhythms – notice how the rhythm of *Wild and wary* changes with each animal. Work out rhythms to characterise other animals – pony, tiger, snake etc.

30

Wild and wary

Hop and stop, hop and stop,
Rabbit sniffs the air
To smell what's there.
Could be danger, could be food,
Could be bad, could be good,
Hop and stop, hop and stop,
Rabbit sniffs the air.

Scurry and flurry and hurry and
 stop,
Squirrel sniffs the air …

Graceful, stately, wary, watching,
Deer sniffs the air …

Snuffly, bumbly, slowly, humbly,
Hedgehog sniffs the air …

Slinky, slidey, creepy, glidey,
Fox sniffs the air …

Verse 1

Verse 2

Verse 3

Verse 4

Verse 5
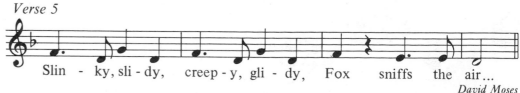

David Moses

Who saw the footprints?

Who saw the footprints in the snow?
Who came along and where did they
   go?

The farmer's wife has just been out
To scatter bits of bread about.
   Who saw the footprints . . .

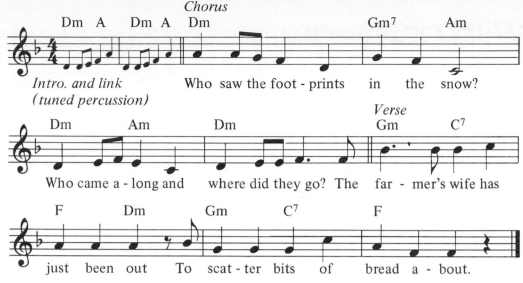

Chorus

Intro. and link
(tuned percussion)

Who saw the foot - prints in the snow?

Verse

Who came a - long and where did they go? The far - mer's wife has

just been out To scat - ter bits of bread a - bout.

Tom Stanier and Elizabeth Bennett

A timid rabbit hopped this way
He sniffed the bread but didn't stay.
   Who saw the footprints . . .

A hungry squirrel found the bread,
Then shivered with cold and went back to bed.
   Who saw the footprints . . .

A deer has tiptoed from the wood
Cautiously to search for food.
   Who saw the footprints . . .

The hedgehog scuffled up at dusk
To drink some milk and nibble a rusk.
   Who saw the footprints . . .

A wary fox in the shadow of night
Finished the bread and was gone by light.

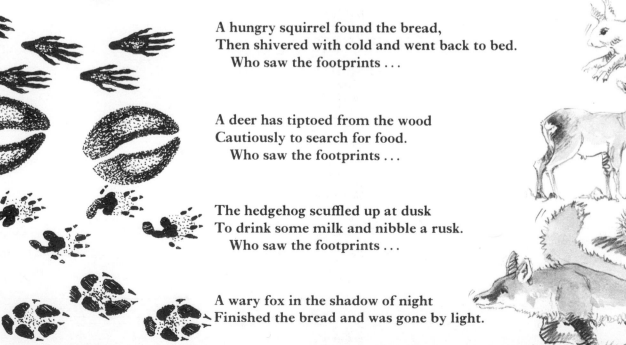

Accompaniment ideas
Tuned percussion

Chorus

Verse

Maracas or shaker filled with dry bread crumbs on 'to scatter bits of bread about'.

Milk bottle top shaker on 'shivered with cold'.

Deer – xylophone, humming, slither box:

mm _____ mm

Activities
Act out the animal movements   *Rabbit* – take several hops, then stop on hind legs to sniff. *Squirrel* – quick, short dashes, pausing on hind legs to sniff. *Deer* – slow, graceful steps, breaking into short runs. *Hedgehog* – scuffling slowly and sniffing the ground. *Fox* – stealthily lifting each paw in turn.

Tracks – make a frieze of tracks using potato cuts and stencils. Discuss the shape of the foot, and how the animals move. Some animals walk on their toes, others on their heels and still others on the flat of their feet. Some run, hop, jump and so on. Add the children's tracks – stand with wellingtons in a tray of paint then walk on paper.

Get the children to experiment making their own footprints in a sandpit. Try out different ways of moving – walking, tiptoeing, hopping, jumping, running fast, limping etc.

Try following tracks made in the playground or, better still, on a country walk. One person goes ahead leaving a trail of crumbs, currants, peanuts, sawdust, or leaves – anything that will disappear naturally later.

Inchworm

Inchworm, inchworm,
Measuring the marigolds,
You and your arithmetic,
You'll probably go far.
Inchworm, inchworm,
Measuring the marigolds,
Seems to me, you'd stop and see
How beautiful they are.

   Two and two are four,
   Four and four are eight,
   Eight and eight are sixteen,
   Sixteen and sixteen are
      thirty-two.
   Two and two are four,
   Four and four are eight,
   Eight and eight are sixteen,
   Sixteen and sixteen are
      thirty-two.

Inchworm, inchworm,
Measuring the marigolds,
You and your arithmetic,
You'll probably go far.
Inchworm, inchworm,
Measuring the marigolds,
Seems to me you'd stop and see
How beautiful they are.

Alternative guitar chords

Capo at third fret

| D | C | D | C | D | G |
| Em7 | A | D | C | D | C |
| D | C | Em7 | A | D | ‖Fine
‖: D | C | D | C | D7 |
| G | D | A7 :‖ D.C. al Fine

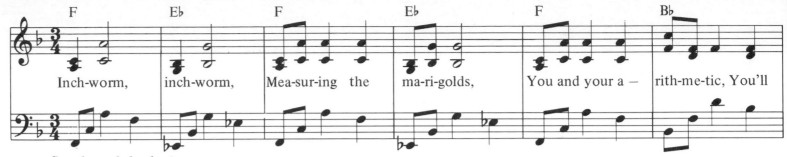

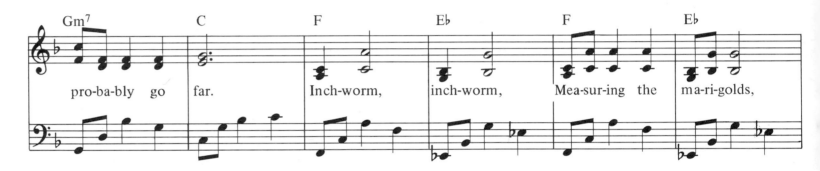

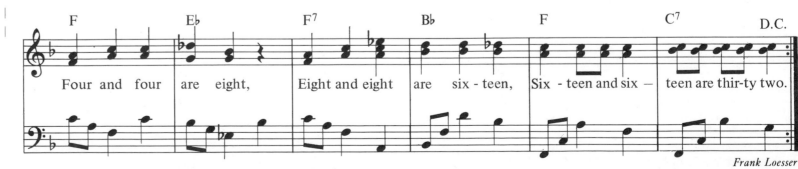

Frank Loesser

Two-part singing

The middle section ('two and two'...) can be sung against the first/last part. Divide into two groups, A and B. Sing in unison through to 'thirty-two', then Group A continues with 'inchworm, inchworm...', while Group B repeats the middle section.

Accompaniment ideas

The rhythm of the music describes the way that the inchworm moves by bunching up its body then stretching it out:

short *long*

Try choosing a dry, short sound for the first beat, and a long stretching sound for the second:

guiro   finger cymbals

Inchworm dance

Make up a dance to the inchworm music, tightening and stretching out. What other activities have a similar rhythm – breaststroke swimming, rowing, climbing a rope, tug of war, pulling on trousers...

Inchworm sack race

The children can pull sacks or dustbin bags up to their waists and tie them, then lie on their tummies and work their way across the floor in time to the song.

Long and short vocal sounds

Make collections of them

short – *click, plop, drip...*

long – *weeee, mooo, aaaaagh...*

Make up a mouth music song using a selection of them.

Match up the rhythms

Write the following words and rhythms on separate cards, then let the children match them up:

walking

galloping

skipping

trotting

skating

Dragon tail

To make the dragon, line up one behind the other with hands on the shoulders of the one in front. The first one in the line is the head and the last is the tip of the tail. On the signal to start, the head swings round and tries to catch the tail. The whole body must move with the head. The children in the middle try to prevent the head from catching the tail.

Mi caballo blanco

As brilliant as the sunrise
My horse is white as snow,
A friend that's ever faithful,
Riding together we will go.
  Mi caballo, mi caballo,
  Galopando va,
  Mi caballo, mi caballo,
  Se vay se va.
  Ah ——————— mm.

On beating wings now flying
In laughter joy and mirth;
Or on sad wings of sorrow,
Lifting me high above the earth.
  Mi caballo, mi caballo . . .

I pray to God in heaven,
For this he sure must know:
When to his side he calls me,
Galloping on my horse I'll go.
  Mi caballo, mi caballo . . .

Caballo pronounced cabal-yo

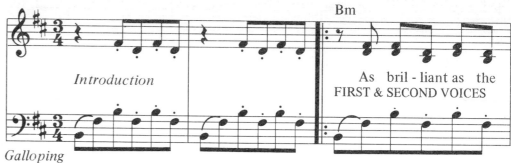

Ah ___

FLUTE, DESCANT RECORDER or THIRD VOICES (one octave lower)

Ah ___

Em — **Bm** — **F#7** — **Bm** — **Em**

Mi ca-bal-lo   mi ca-bal-lo   Ga-lo- pan- do va,   Mi ca-ballo,

Mi ca-bal-lo,   mi ca-bal-lo

Bm — **F#7** — **Bm** — **D** — **A**

mi ca- bal-lo,   Se vay   se va.   Ah ___

last time

mi ca- bal-lo,   ga- lo-pan-do va. ___

G — **F#7** — **Bm**

mm ___

Francisco Floro del Campo, English words by Timothy Roberts

Accompaniment ideas

Try playing a trotting rhythm in the verse and a galloping rhythm in the chorus:

Trotting: woodblock, yoghurt pots, or coconut shells:

Galloping: scraper and tambour with soft stick:

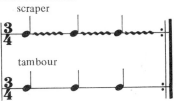

scraper

tambour

Activities

Gaits – the sequence in which a horse places its hooves on the ground changes according to whether it is walking, trotting or galloping:

	3 4			1 2
Walking	⟶		*Trotting*	⟶
	1 2			2 1

	2 4			2 3
Transverse	⟶		*Rotary*	⟶
gallop	1 3		*gallop*	1 4

Look at the sequence in which other animals move their legs. Examine animals like centipedes, beetles, and birds as well as other four-legged animals.

Physical adaptations – look into the ways in which animals are specially adapted physically to help them move, e.g. swimming birds have webbed feet, or paddle-shaped toes, antelopes have small light hooves for running fast, moles have velvety coats so that they can move forwards and backwards through their tunnels without turning round, bats have claws on their wings for climbing, desert woodlice have long legs for running on tiptoe over burning hot sand.

Farmer in the fog

Basic use

Sing it as written, and add more animals.

Play it as a ring game

Write out the name of each animal on a card and give one to each child. One of the cards is left blank and the child who gets this is the farmer. Blindfold the farmer and form a ring round him or her. Sing the song. The person who has the cat card sings the *meows* and from this the farmer has to locate and touch her. Repeat the line 'He listened and he heard *meow meow meow*' until the cat is found, then go on to the next verse, until all the animals have had their turn.

Add more animals if there are not enough, or double them up so that the farmer has to find a flock of sheep or a herd of cows! The farmer can change places with one of the animals he finds to give others a turn.

Gamekeeper in the fog

Find out about the sounds that wild creatures make and change the song to *Gamekeeper in the fog*. (The picture-book *Gobble Growl Grunt* by Peter Spier is a good source of animal sounds, but look for recordings as well – or make your own at the zoo!)

Oh the farmer said, I've lost my cat,
She's small and black, goes *meow meow meow.*
It's a foggy day and I've lost my way,
I'll follow the sound of *meow meow meow.*
Sh – sh – sh sh sh
　So he listened and he heard
　　meow meow meow
　He listened and he heard
　　meow meow meow.
Then the farmer said, I've found my cat,
But now I've lost my dog!

Oh the farmer said, I've lost my dog,
He's got a long tail, goes *woof woof woof* . . .
Then the farmer said, I've found my dog,
But now I've lost my cow.

Oh the farmer said, I've lost my cow,
She's big and brown, goes *moo moo moo* . . .
Then the farmer said, I've found my cow,
But now I've lost my pig.

Oh the farmer said, I've lost my pig,
He's fat and pink, goes *oink oink oink* . . .
Then the farmer said, I've found my pig,
But now I've lost my sheep.

Oh the farmer said, I've lost my sheep,
She's woolly and white, goes *baa baa baa* . . .
Then the farmer said,
　I've found my sheep,
　found my pig, found my cow,
　found my dog, found my cat,
　and the farmer said, that's that!

With a slow swing

Accompaniment ideas

The song needs to be uncluttered, particularly if you are playing the ring game. A guitar is very suitable and you might add:

Maraca played very softly at *sh sh* . . .

Tambourine at

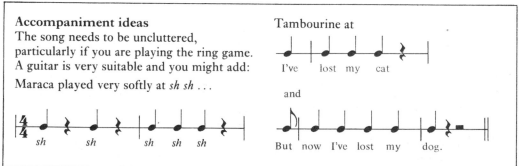

36

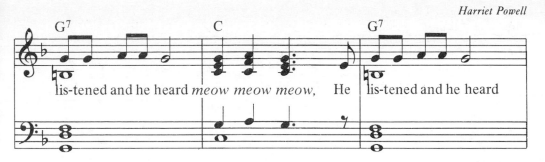

Harriet Powell

Noah's ark

Make a list of animals half as long as the number of players, then write the name of each animal on two separate cards. Shuffle the pack and deal one card out to each player, who must look to see what animal they are then return it, keeping their identity secret.

The animals now have to find their mates. They are not allowed to speak but they may make any sound or action they like, as long as it is characteristic of their animal.

On a signal from the leader, everyone starts to growl, croak, screech, strut, flap, leap and pose in order to identify themselves to their mate.

Alternative guitar chords

Capo on third fret

D	G A	G A	G A
D	G A	G A	A D	A —	—
E₇	A	E₇	A A₇
D	G A	A	D	

Link – use the following as chords for guitar or notes for tuned percussion (start on the first beat of the last bar – on 'dog'.)

After verse 2 add *woof woof woof woof*, and so on until all the animals have joined in.

Alternatively build up an accumulation of percussion sounds playing the same rhythm: cat – jingles, dog – woodblock, cow – tambour, pigs – guiro, sheep – clappers.

Add to this an accumulation of the sounds from each verse, i.e. after verse 1:

Roar, lion, roar

One person is chosen to be blindfolded and to stand in the centre of a ring formed by the others. Everyone dances round to music (recorder playing *Farmer in the fog*, perhaps?) until the person in the centre shouts 'stop', points to the ring and says, 'Roar, lion, roar' (or 'Moo, cow, moo', or any other animal). The child pointed to must roar, and the blindfolded child must guess who is roaring. If the guess is correct the other child takes a turn in the centre.

The broomsquire's birdsong

Accompaniment ideas

A pentatonic melody (on the notes G A B D E), which needs only the lightest accompaniment, if any. Try repeating a chord of DGD very softly in the highest register of the piano or on glockenspiel or chime bars throughout:

A drone of the same notes could be played on violin, cello or guitar.

Tambour or small drum and wooden beater (tap very softly)

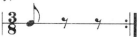

Activities

How many birds? In the school grounds, or if possible, in a forest, meadow, or park, get the children (in small groups) to lie down on their backs with both fists in the air. Every time someone hears a new birdsong, he or she lifts one finger.

During the listening period, get someone else to make a recording so that afterwards you can all refer to it, and check which species were singing and calling.

Birds produce their songs and calls from a special voice box called the syrinx at the bottom of the windpipe, not at the top, like ours. Every species has a distinctive song vocabulary, which we can use to identify them. There is a difference between singing and calling. A song may be a very elaborate series of sounds. It is used particularly by male birds to proclaim territory, warn off other males and attract females, and to bond pairs. Whereas a call may be very short, and may be used to warn others of danger (as in the alarm calls given in the story opposite), to advertise a feast of food to others, to maintain contact within flocks of migrating birds, or to let a parent bird know that its baby is ready for the next mouthful.

Of all the birds that ever I see,
The colley-bird's song is the finest for me.
The dove she croons for she'd sing if she could,
The old cock pheasant, he crows in the wood.
The bullfinch pipes in the orchard tree,
But the colley-bird's song is the finest for me.
The small Jenny wren, she has a loud song,
The tits and the sparrows they all go along,
The hen, she cackles again and again,
But the colley-bird, the colley-bird carols after the rain.

The curlew, he cries far out on the hill,
The rooks and the jackdaws let go with a will,
The nightingale sings in the still of the night,
The thrush he hails the morning light,
The linnet he goes it so sweet do he,
But the colley-bird's song is the finest for me.
The missel, he calls when the storm be strong,
The ruddick, he cheers us when winter be long,
The duck she quackles and quackles so plain,
But the colley-bird, the colley-bird carols after the rain.

Of all — the birds that e-ver I see, The col-ley bird's song is the fi-nest for me. The

Rhythmic and lyrical

dove she croons for she'd sing if she could, The old__ cock phea-sant, he crows in the wood. The

bull - finch pipes_ in the or__ chard tree, But the col - ley bird's song is the fi - nest for me. The

small Jen-ny wren, she has a loud song, The tits and the spar-rows they all go a — long, The hen, she

cackles a — gain and a — gain, But the col-ley bird, the col-ley bird ca-rols af - ter the rain.

Broomsquire – gypsy *Colley-bird* – blackbird *Missel* – missel thrush *Ruddick* – robin   *Traditional English: collected by Ruth Tongue*

The blue tits and the cat
A sound story for descant recorders and piano

Preparation – the recorder players need to practise trills, and also flutter-tonguing, which is achieved by saying *trrrr* while blowing into the recorder.

① It is a summer day in an English garden. A group of blue tits arrive, some of them perching on branches, while others feed at the bird table. They begin to sing to let everyone know they are there:

accelerando...

Recorder players – repeat each of these phrases two or three times, but leave long gaps between repeats. Play the phrases in any order – everyone should be playing different ones at once. Play independently.

② After some time a cat comes into the garden and moves very quietly towards the bird table:

③ When the blue tits first spot the cat they give out an alarm call to warn the other birds (i). As the cat gets closer the alarm calls become more intense (ii).

Recorder players – introduce the first alarm call into your birdsong phrases gradually. Then, as the piano's phrases become more threatening, begin to play the second alarm call.

Piano – play these phrases quietly while the birdsong continues.

④ At last, the cat leaps at one of the blue tits, but he cannot catch it.

Recorder players – keep playing the alarm calls until you hear the last piano chord, then stop.

Suddenly all the birds fly off and the garden is left in silence.

Peter Stacey

The lost hippos

Sue Beer

Preparation

You will need a) two hippos b) a group of instrumentalists to accompany their song (piano, tuned and untuned percussion) c) groups of monkeys, birds, crocodiles and fish.

The groups of animals should each, after discussion, choose instruments to represent themselves, e.g. the birds might decide to use recorders, or a small glockenspiel, the crocodiles might choose clappers and scrapers, and so on (let the children choose a different selection of animals if they like).

Position each group of animals in different parts of the 'forest' – a large room or hall.

Musical points to be aware of
Spend some time discussing and experimenting with the choice of instruments which are to represent the animals. Think carefully about how to use the sounds – should they be random or rhythmic, what special techniques might be used (trills, glissandi etc)? Try to convey things about the animal's character, movements and habitat, as well as vocal sounds.

Point out the contrast between the loud and soft versions of the hippos' song (*f* and *p*). Encourage the hippos to move in different ways – thumping and crashing loudly, then tiptoeing quietly.

Note the use of *crescendo* (getting louder) as the hippos get nearer to a group of animals, and *decrescendo* (getting softer) as they get further away.

Two hippos are wallowing in their mudhole. It is very hot and they are very bored! They decide to go for a walk in the forest to find their friends. Off they go (accompanied by the *Crash crash bang* song).

Soon they come to a group of monkeys chattering in the trees. (Monkeys make their sounds as the hippos approach.) They pass the time of day, (improvise some small talk), then the hippos set off again. (*Crash crash bang*.)

Next they meet some birds singing and calling to each other high up in the tree-tops. (Birds make their sounds.) Then they find crocodiles lazing on the river bank. (Crocodile sounds.) Lastly they meet a shoal of fish playing in a pool below a small waterfall. (Fish and water sounds.) The hippos wander on.

By now they are tired, but when they turn homewards they discover that they don't know where they are. They sit down to decide what to do. 'I know,' says one, 'if we're very quiet, we might be able to hear the last group of friends we passed.'

Sure enough, in the distance, they hear a faint sound of the fish, and they set off towards them. (*Sh sh sh* song.) The fish sounds get louder until the hippos find themselves by the waterfall again. Next they all listen for the sounds of the crocodiles and hear them in the distance. As they approach the crocodiles, the fish sounds become more distant and the crocodiles become louder. They find the river bank again and on they go, listening in turn for the birds, and finally the monkeys. At last, exhausted, they reach their mudhole, flop down and quickly fall asleep.

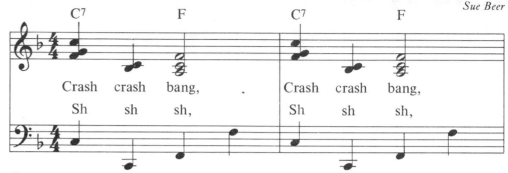

First time: heavily
Second time: softly

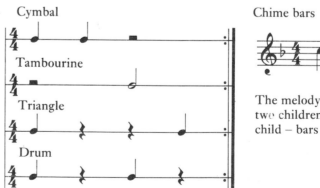

The melody line can be played by one or two children on tuned percussion (first child – bars 1, 2 and 4; second child – bar 3).

40

Rillaby rill

Traditional

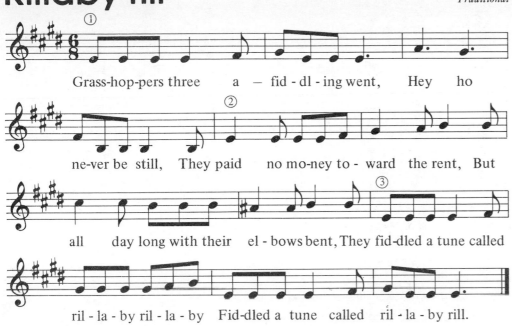

Grass-hop-pers three a – fid-dl-ing went, Hey ho

ne-ver be still, They paid no mo-ney to - ward the rent, But

all day long with their el - bows bent, They fid-dled a tune called

ril - la - by ril - la - by Fid-dled a tune called ril - la - by rill.

Accompaniment ideas
Scrapers – experiment with different materials to find three contrasting scraping sounds – soft, medium and loud, e.g. a comb scraped with a pencil tip or hairgrip, a piece of corrugated paper scraped with finger nails, a guiro or ridged plastic bottle. Let each scraper play different rhythm patterns from the melody:

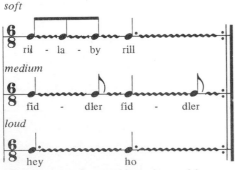

soft — ril - la - by rill
medium — fid - dler fid - dler
loud — hey ho

The song can be sung in unison with the three-scraper accompaniment, or as a round, the second and third voices (or grasshoppers!) joining in after four and eight bars respectively. A round is often based on one chord. This round is based on two, and some strong clashes are produced between the voices – rather like grasshoppers sawing away at different pitches! Use the loudest scraper for accompaniment.

Activities
Communicating with non-vocal sounds – grasshoppers and locusts rub their legs against their bodies; cicadas, the loudest insect 'singers' vibrate an inner wall of their abdomen making it click like the lid of a biscuit tin – up to 600 times a second. Woodpeckers drum on wood, woodcocks vibrate their tail feathers, some fish vibrate their swim bladders. Investigate other non-vocal sound makers and find out what and how they communicate.

Giraffe semaphore

Giraffes move their ears about in a kind of semaphore which they use for communicating with one another. Divide the children into family groups of giraffes – adults and young. One adult giraffe is chosen to be leader and initiates all the signals:

"NO MESSAGE." (move around eating leaves off tall trees.)

"GO AWAY AND LEAVE ME ALONE" (Spread out to the furthest corners of the room)

"I'M INTERESTED IN YOU" (Touch noses)

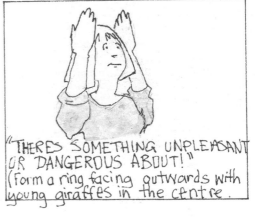

"THERE'S SOMETHING UNPLEASANT OR DANGEROUS ABOUT!" (Form a ring facing outwards with young giraffes in the centre.

Bat and moth

Form a circle of children, ten to fifteen feet across. Choose one person to be the bat, and position him or her, blindfolded, in the centre of the ring. Pick out two or three other children to be moths, who can move about anywhere inside the circle.

The bat has to try to catch the moths and uses 'radar' to help. To do this the bat calls out 'bat', and every time they hear this, the moths call back 'moth'. The bat's cry is his radar signal, which bounces off the moths and returns to him in their cries. Having located their position he needs to move quickly in for the kill!

41

Body language

Introduction

If you're happy or angry or feeling blue,
There are plenty of things that you can do:
You can laugh or cry, you can scowl,
    or say,
'I'm cross!' or 'Wow! what a wonderful day!'
But, what do the animals do?
Yes! What do the animals do?

Chorus

Body language is the name of the game.
Body language, can we all do the same?
Stand still, and sniff, wave your tail
    around,
Let your hair stand up on end, and stamp
    upon the ground.
For that's what the animals do,
Yes, that's what the animals do.

Verse (insert animal of your choice)

Here's a cat to say hello.
Have a good look, is it friend or foe?
I'm the boss, I'm strong, I've a dominant
    streak,
I'd like to be friends, but I'm little
    and weak.
We think we'll get along fine,
Yes, we think we'll get along fine.

Veronica Clark

This is a game song for acting out animal body language. Before starting, discuss and rehearse the body language you are going to act out in the song. How do two cats behave when they meet each other? Which other animals are you going to sing about? Elephants, monkeys and dogs, are some of the easier ones to try (see the examples given opposite). Think about the purpose of body language in this kind of situation, i.e. where two animals meet – what does the posturing help to prevent? Talk about a wide variety of animals, and different situations, though you won't be able to use all of them in the song – many are impossible to mime! How do *we* use body language? (Ref. *Manwatching* by Desmond Morris).

The action

The children form pairs and decide which is going to be the dominant animal and which the weaker one. Next, form two lines, with a large space between, and with pairs facing each other. (If preferred, pairs can take turns to act out different animals, while the others sing and accompany on instruments.)

Introduction

Make suitably happy or sad or angry faces in response to the words.

Chorus

Lines 1–2: move forward taking four small steps per line. Walk in an animal-like way, but standing upright – use the hands like paws to imitate a creeping movement. (If space is limited, stand still and simply pretend to move towards the other line – waving paws in the air.)

Lines 3–4: act out the words – stand still, sniff the air, use an arm as a tail and wave it around behind the back, pull up the hair with the hands, and finally stamp three times.

Lines 5–6: move backwards to the starting place, wagging a knowledgeable finger in time to the beat.

Verse – cat

Lines 1–2: acknowledge each other from a distance, moving slowly towards each other rather stiffly and cautiously.

Line 3: the dominant cat postures aggressively arching its back and advancing slowly but boldly.

Line 4: the weaker cat becomes submissive, backing off slightly, turning to expose one side, avoiding eye contact, and cringeing a little.

Lines 5–6: friendly greetings – the dominant cat touches the other's nose with his.

Link – during the first two lines of the chorus, the two lines move back to their starting points.

Threatening, dominant postures

Elephant – swings lowered head and trunk from side to side, ears spread out to side.

Dog – teeth bared and muzzle wrinkled in snarl, steady gaze, ears and tail erect, taut muscles and erect stance.

Monkey – mouth opened wide with bared teeth.

Submissive, frightened postures

Elephant – trunk curled right up to mouth, ears flattened.

Dog – tail curled between legs, ears flattened back, eyes avoiding gaze, shivering, hesitant, crouching stance, exposing side or rolling on back.

Monkey – avoiding eye contact, shuffling backwards with head turned away, holding another's hand for reassurance.

Greetings

Elephant – shakes trunk with other elephant

Dog – wags tail and touches nose to nose.

Monkey – friendly faces and hand touching.

43

Hide!

A game song – sing it as here, then make up new verses. You can build several verses into a food chain as in the beetle – mole – fox example given here.

Choose an animal such as an earthworm, and ask the children what other animal would eat it – what is its predator? They might suggest a blackbird. Sing the verse, then pause before the chorus to ask where the earthworm would hide. Before the start of the next verse ask them what might try to catch and eat a blackbird, and so on.

Variation – change the form of defence. Think of other ways in which animals escape from predators, e.g. by giving a fierce warning (as in *The Cobra and the Yogi*), by camouflaging themselves, by protecting themselves with armour (hedgehog, tortoise), or by flight – running, jumping, flying, hopping, swimming. See if you can make up verses using these themes, e.g.

   If I were an antelope, grazing around
   Grazing around, grazing around,
   And along came a cheetah,
   What would I do?
   RUN! Well wouldn't you?
     Run, run, run! Run, run, run!
     Over the ground, like a streak of
      light,
     Keep on running till I'm out of
      sight,
     Hi there, cheetah! You can't catch
      me!
   (*shout gleefully*)

If I was a beetle, beetling around,
Beetling around, beetling around,
And along came a mole,
What would I do?
HIDE! Well, wouldn't you?
   Hide, hide, hide! Hide, hide, hide!
   Underneath a stone, safe inside.
   Keep very still, *sh*, hee hee hee,
   Hi there, mole! You can't catch me!
(*Whisper gleefully*)

If I was a mole, scuttling around,
Scuttling around, scuttling around,
And along came a fox,
What would I do?
HIDE! Well, wouldn't you?
   Hide, hide, hide! Hide, hide, hide!
   Underneath the ground, safe inside.
   Keep very still, *sh*, hee hee hee,
   Hi there, fox! You can't catch me!

If I was a fox, scurrying around,
Scurrying around, scurrying around,
And along came the hounds,
What would I do?
HIDE! Well, wouldn't you?
   Hide, hide, hide! Hide, hide, hide!
   Underneath the ground, safe inside.
   Keep very still, *sh*, hee hee hee,
   Hi there, hounds! You can't catch me!

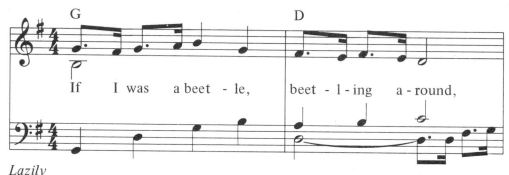

Lazily

Faster

Creep, mouse, creep! The old cat lies a – sleep; The

Stealthy

dog's a – way, The kit-tens play; Creep, mouse, creep!

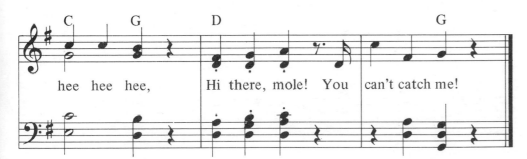

Un – der-neath a stone, safe in – side. Keep ve – ry still, sh, *pp*

hee hee hee, Hi there, mole! You can't catch me!

Harriet Powell

TUNED PERCUSSION (and alternative guitar chords)

Accompaniment ideas

A very light accompaniment is needed to allow for pausing to improvise new verses.

Bars 1–6: tuned percussion outlining the melody.

Bars 7–8: indicate a squeal of fear then shivering, with a short, sharp blow through a recorder mouthpiece, then a shaken tambourine or maraca:

recorder   shaker

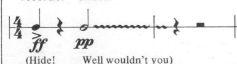

ff   *pp*

(Hide!   Well wouldn't you)

Bars 9–12: cymbal tapped with a wooden beater

Bars 13–14: maraca

(Keep very still   hee hee hee)

Bars 15–16: tambourine tapped in the rhythm of the words.

(Hi there, mole! You can't catch me!)

A game of stealth. One child is chosen to be the cat and curls up in the centre of a ring, which the others form as they creep round pretending to be mice and making as little noise as possible. As soon as the verse ends the cat leaps up and tries to catch a mouse. You can make one area of the room the mice's den, where if they can get to it they are safe. Whoever is caught becomes a cat and helps to catch the remaining mice.

Variation – Blindfold the cat and give him a torch. The cat sits in the middle of the room and all the mice must pass in front of him to get from one side to the other. Sing the song and the mice start to move. When the song ends, the mice must move in total silence. If the cat hears a sound, he may shine his torch in the direction he thinks it came from – if a mouse is caught in the beam, he must go back to the start. (No wild waving of the torch is allowed. Darken the room if necessary.)

Accompaniment ideas

Think of some really soft sounds to use as accompaniment to the creeping mouse – rustling paper, a triangle, a small matchbox filled with rice, fingernails scratching the skin of a tambour.

(Encourage the children to observe the rests in the music. Tell them that you are going to drop a pin during one of the rests, and ask them to put up their hands when they hear it fall.)

Tambour very softly tapped with hand all through.

You can't make a turtle come out

Animals use a variety of protective coverings. Some just have tough leathery skin, which is often scaly, e.g. fish, reptiles, elephants, rhinos, hippos. The thickness of the skin is the main protection. Other animals use prickles or quills. These may be moveable as in porcupines, sea urchins, some caterpillars; or may be fixed, though the animals can still curl up as with the hedgehog.

Armour plating is usually jointed to allow movement, e.g. crabs, lobsters, woodlice, armadillos, crocodiles. Sometimes it is a rigid shell into which the animal can pull itself, e.g. tortoise, turtle, snail.

Activities

Armour design – ask the children to design and draw themselves a protective covering for defence against an imaginary predator. Discuss which are the most vulnerable parts needing the best protection, and the importance of allowing for movement. Discuss the advantages and drawbacks of their designs.

Draw a fantasy creature with an impregnable defensive covering. Allow a full range of possibilities – horns, spikes, armour plates, scales. Discuss the advantages and disadvantages of the different kinds of protective covering – e.g. rigidity, weight, lack of speed for catching prey, as opposed to lack of predators, and so on. Compare the defences of an impregnable herbivore such as a rhinoceros, with the defences of an impregnable predator like a polar bear.

You can't make a turtle come out,
You can't make a turtle come out,
You can coax him or call him
   or shake him or shout,
But you can't make a turtle come out,
   come out,
You can't make a turtle come out.

If he wants to stay in his shell,
If he wants to stay in his shell,
You can knock on the door,
   but you can't ring the bell,
And you can't make a turtle come out,
   come out,
You can't make a turtle come out.

Be kind to your four-footed friends,
Be kind to your four-footed friends,
A poke makes a turtle retreat at
   both ends,
And you can't make a turtle come out,
   come out,
You can't make a turtle come out.

So you'll have to patiently wait,
So you'll have to patiently wait,
And when he gets ready, he'll open
   the gate,
But you can't make a turtle come out,
   come out,
You can't make a turtle come out.

And when you forget that he's there,
And when you forget that he's there,
He'll be walking around with his head
   in the air,
But you can't make a turtle come out,
   come out,
You can't make a turtle come out.

With a gentle swing

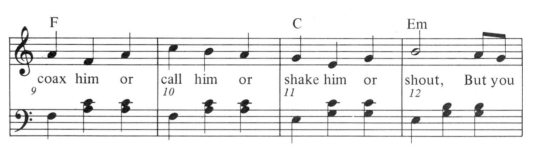

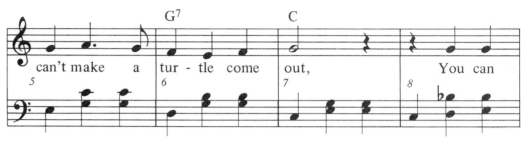

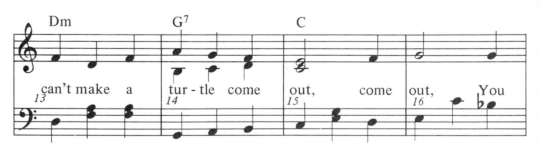

can't make a tur-tle come out.

TUNED PERCUSSION (e.g. bass xylophone)

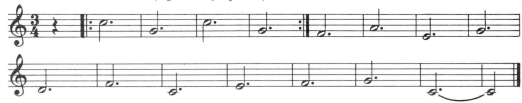

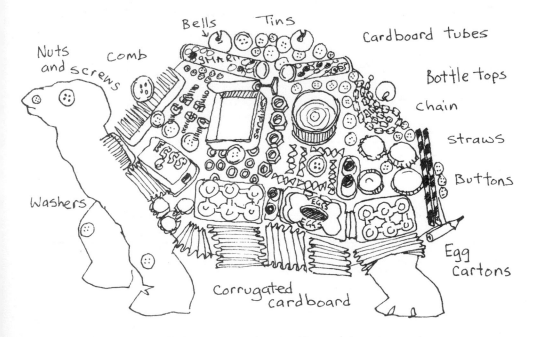

Nuts and screws

Comb

Bells

Tins

Cardboard tubes

Bottle tops

Chain

Straws

Buttons

Washers

Egg Cartons

Corrugated cardboard

Heavy Duty Cardboard Animal.

Accompaniment ideas

Hard tapping sounds can give an impression of the turtle's tough shell, and scraping sounds can give an idea of the texture. Build up the sounds progressively in the first and last part of the verse, e.g.

Lines 1–2 and 5–6 (bars 1–8 and 13–20)

Verse 1

Bass tambour   Snare drum

etc.

Verse 2 – add scraper:

Verse 3 – add woodblock:

Verse 4 – add large bass drum, cardboard box, or oil drum:

Verse 5 – no unpitched percussion. Use a soprano glockenspiel for the tuned percussion part.

Lines 3–4 (bars 9–12)

Try adding various sound effects to this middle section, e.g.

Verse 1 – maraca on 'shake', shout 'shout'.

Verse 2 – woodblock on 'knock on the door', bicycle bell or voice saying *brrr* on 'ring the bell'.

Verse 3 – squeaky toy on 'poke', tambour on 'both ends'.

Verse 4 – swanee whistle (push slide in) on 'gate'.

Verse 5 – play the tuned percussion part on soprano glockenspiel, and whistle the tune at 'he'll be walking around with his head in the air.'

Activities

Make a fantasy turtle sound-sculpture.
First collect together materials which will make hard, tough or dry sounds – metal tins, washers, plastic egg cartons, corrugated paper, milk bottle tops, tinfoil plates, cardboard tubes, pasta shapes, buttons and so on.

Then make a large turtle (or rhino, or dragon) cut out from heavy duty cardboard, or pegboard, and glue, tie and pin on securely your collection of sound makers. Suspend the structure, or attach it to a wall, and play it with the hands, or with a variety of beaters (see below).

Hard and soft beaters – discuss how you can alter the sounds that percussion instruments make by using different kinds of beaters. Make a wide variety of hard beaters from different materials:

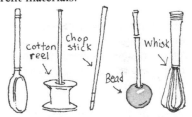

cotton reel

chop stick

Bead

whisk

Do the same with soft beaters:

carpet

cotton wool

rubber

Try all these out on one instrument, to see how many different sounds can be made, and how they contrast.

This song calls for hard beaters. Look for another in the book which calls for soft beaters and contrast the two – try swapping the beaters, using soft ones in *You can't make a turtle come out*, and vice versa with the other song – talk about the effect.

Never smile at a crocodile

Never smile at a crocodile,
No, you can't get friendly with a crocodile;
Don't be taken in by his welcome grin,
He's imagining how well you'd fit within his skin.
Never smile at a crocodile,
Never tip your hat and stop to talk awhile.
Never run, walk away,
Say 'Good night,' not 'Good day!'
Clear the aisle and never smile at Mr Crocodile.

You may very well be well bred,
Lots of etiquette in your head,
But there's always some special case,
Time or place, to forget etiquette.
For instance –

Never smile at a crocodile,
No, you can't get friendly with a crocodile;
Don't be taken in by his welcome grin,
He's imagining how well you'd fit within his skin.
Never smile at a crocodile,
Never tip your hat and stop to talk awhile.
Don't be rude, never mock,
Throw a kiss, not a rock.
Clear the aisle and never smile at Mr Crocodile.

Jack Lawrence and Frank Churchill

Ne - ver smile at a cro - co - dile, Ne-ver tip your hat and stop to talk a - while Ne-ver

run, walk a - way, say "Good night", not "Good day" Clear the aisle and ne-ver smile at Mis-ter Cro - co - dile.

Interlude

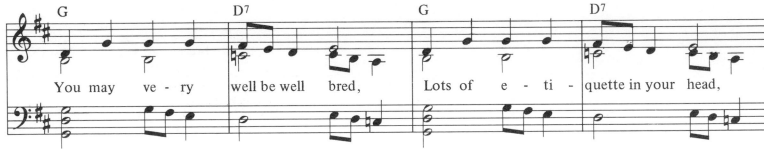

You may ve - ry well be well bred, Lots of e - ti - quette in your head,

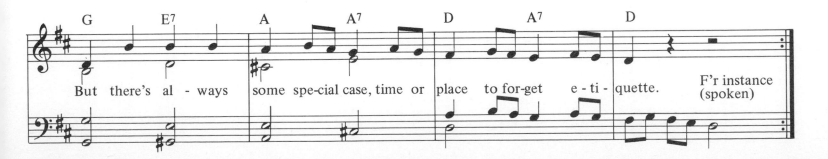

But there's al - ways some spe-cial case, time or place to for-get e - ti - quette. F'r instance (spoken)

Accompaniment ideas
Bars 1–12

Tambour

Clappers/ruler

Bars 13–16

Tambourine tapped lightly

Like the polar bear, rhinoceros, elephant, lion, tiger, whale, and other large species whose defence is their sheer size or ferocity, the crocodile has no predators except well-armed humans.

49

The yogi and the cobra

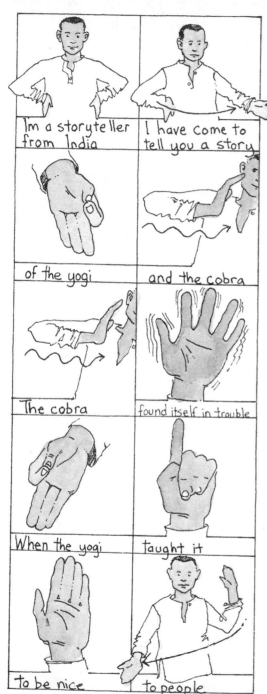

Singers

**I'm a storyteller from India,
I have come to tell you
The story of the yogi and the cobra,
Story of the yogi and the cobra.
Cobra found itself in trouble
When the yogi taught it to be nice
to people.**

Narrator

There once lived a fierce cobra inside a hedge near a town. Children used to play in the fields nearby. But the cobra was a menace, killing and injuring many animals and people. Everyone lived in fear of it, and the children were afraid to pass that way to go to the fields.

One day a wise man, a yogi, walked through the town. The people warned him not to pass by the hedge — "A cobra lives there and it is sure to kill you." But the yogi was not put off that easily, and walked towards the dreaded place. Suddenly, the cobra shot out, raised its hood to strike its deathly blow — but stopped. The yogi stood still and calm. He didn't try to run, and for a moment the cobra wondered if he was alive. The the yogi knelt in front of the cobra and began to speak: "Why do you have to kill people and injure them? You must lead a peaceful life and let others live around you. I shall teach you the name of the Lord, so that you may take it and live in peace."

It was an overwhelming experience for the cobra. It quietened down and decided to change. It learned to find peace and happiness in itself.

I'm a sto-ry-tel-ler from In — di-a.___

I have come to tell you the sto-ry of the Yo-gi and the co-bra.___

Co-bra found it-self in trou-ble___ when the Yo-gi taught it to be

Instrumental interlude

nice to peo-ple.

Preparation

This is an Indian song story. You will need a narrator, a group of singers and dancers (or five groups – one to each section of the song), and a group of instrumentalists.

The dancers mime the story during the song sections. Try to make the actions flow into each other without a break. Move the whole body as well as the hands: step sideways at 'I'm a storyteller,' prance from side to side at 'playful boys,' advance, sway, or cringe back to emphasise the actions.

Accompaniment ideas

The singing needs to be rhythmic to help the dancers. A percussion accompaniment can be improvised on two-toned drums, using the rhythms of the melody. A drone can be played throughout on instruments such as violins, cellos or tuned percussion using these notes in varied patterns:

At the end of each section, play the interlude on recorder or tuned percussion. The scale can be played in free rhythm to make it easier, but it needs to be quite emphatic to give the effect of a flourish.

A co-bra, vis-cious and ter-ri-ble,

killed a-ni-mals and peo-ple. ___

A wise yo-gi came and taught the

co-bra to be peace-ful.

Play-ful boys came from the town, and

beat the co-bra___ down. The co-bra crawled___ in-

side___ the ground; ate no-thing___ till by

yo-gi it was found.

Singers

A cobra, vicious and terrible,
Killed animals and people.
A cobra, vicious and terrible,
Killed animals and people.
A wise yogi came and taught
The cobra to be peaceful.

Narrator

The people were glad that the cobra was no longer a menace, and the children played happily in the fields again. Soon, some wicked boys of the town decided to visit the cobra and see for themselves how quiet it had become. At first they were scared, then, when the cobra did nothing, they approached closer and closer until they could reach out and touch it. Boldly, they stroked its head as it lay on the rock enjoying the new peace it had found. And even when they held the cobra by its neck there was not a whisper, not a wriggle of protest. One of the boys suggested it might be fun to thrash the cobra against the rock, so the poor cobra found itself mercilessly beaten. Quietly it crawled into its hole, and lay there not daring to come out even to eat.

A year went by and the yogi returned. He was certain he would find the cobra living happily and peacefully, but to his great surprise, it was nowhere to be seen. When at last he found the cobra hidden away in its hole, it was as thin as a skeleton, and very nearly dead.

Singers

Playful boys came from the town,
And beat the cobra down.
The cobra crawled inside the ground;
Ate nothing till by the yogi it was found.

Narrator

Then the yogi fed the cobra with milk and honey and it began to revive. Then he asked, "How have you got like this?".The cobra whispered, "You taught me to become very peaceful. Before I knew where I was I was dragged and beaten by the wicked boys of the town."

The yogi was shocked. "But I only told you not to kill!" he exclaimed.

Singers

The yogi fed the cobra
And made it well again.
In dismay he exclaimed,
I told you only not to kill.

Narrator

Then the yogi said, "I didn't tell you not to frighten your enemies away – I did not tell you not to hiss!"

Singers

To act in self defence,
To scare the enemy away,
Did I tell you you may not
Raise your hood and hiss?
Did I tell you you may not
Raise your hood and hisssss.

The North Wind blows
Soundtrack for a wildlife film

The scenario – it is September in the Arctic tundra, and the North Wind steals out to chill the air below freezing. (High-pitched whistling over the tops of pen lids, fingers run round and round the wet rims of wine glasses.)

The snow geese are the first to notice the new chill. They gather in huge flocks, rising from the water in great clapping clouds of wings. (Wooden clappers, sheets of paper flapped and scrumpled, wire brush and cymbal.) Suddenly their journey begins, and they leave the marshes and lakes, flying southwards in v-shaped formations. The warmth of the south calls to them. (Warmth theme – soft beaters rubbed across the bars of a metallophone, low drone on cello.)

Stronger now, and more insistent and menacing, the North Wind turns on the group of lemmings. They respond with a flurry of activity, first scratching at the surface of the earth, then scrabbling deeper and deeper to build a labyrinth of tunnels and warm nests. (Hurrying ostinato figures on glockenspiel, sandpaper blocks rubbed together, scrapers.) Again the North Wind is left behind as the lemmings nestle together and listen to the gale outside. (Warmth theme.)

The wind builds itself into a furious blizzard. (Shakers filled with rice or grit, wine glasses, high shrill notes on recorders, cymbal and hard beater, undulating vocal sounds.) One by one the musk oxen move together to form a circle. (Long slow beats on a gong, or sustained, repeated bass chords on piano.) Inside the circle, sheltering in the relative calm, stand a group of youngsters. (Warmth theme.)

The blizzard passes over and the North Wind dies away, leaving the animals unconquered.

Preparation – divide into five groups, one to each of the following parts – the *North Wind* (main theme), *Snow geese* (first episode) *Lemmings* (second episode), *Musk oxen* (third episode), *Warmth* (mini-theme).

Each group needs to discuss how to create their part in the composition, which is to be the soundtrack for a wildlife film. Encourage them to draw from a wide palette of sounds and playing techniques, including homemade instruments, vocal and body sounds. A few suggestions are given but ignore them if they are not needed.

Background
Snow geese spend summer in the Arctic tundra – vast expanses of treeless, low-growing vegetation, lakes and marshes, which in winter are covered by ice and snow. In September they fly south to warmer climates.

In winter, lemmings dig into the ground and make nests of rough grass about a metre below the surface. The lemming's body heat keeps the nest at a comfortable 10°, well above the freezing temperatures outside.

The musk ox's coat of dense, soft wool overlaid by thick guard hairs reaching to the ground, is its winter protection. In severe cold, adult musk oxen form a circle shoulder to shoulder, heads facing outward, to form a shelter for their young.

Musical points to consider
a) The children need to think how to join the sections into one piece of music – the constant crescendo of the North Wind, linking the three contrasting episodes which describe the animals' different responses to the cold, and the recurring warmth theme. How will they merge? Do you need a conductor? Should there be a spoken commentary? b) How might the composition be notated, both in overall shape and detail?

Winter food stores

Oh dear, what shall we do?
Winter's coming and we've got no food.

If I were a hamster looking for grain,
I wouldn't mind the wind and I wouldn't mind the rain.
I'd search around on the woodland floor,
And I'd stuff my face until I couldn't eat another
    bit more.
    Oh dear, what shall we do . . .

If I were a bee I'd look for honey,
Get sticky yellow pollen on my legs and tummy.
I'd search the flowers and I'd search them well,
Then back to the hive, store my honey in a waxy cell.
    Oh dear, what shall we do . . .

If I were a dormouse, I'd like best
A pile of furry beech nuts hidden in my nest.
I'd hurry back home bringing all I'd found
And bury my treasure deep down in my burrow underground.
    Oh dear, what shall we do . . .

If I were a mole, I'd look for a worm.
I'd listen, then I'd dig as it wriggled and it squirmed.
I'd gather up worms for all I was worth,
Then I'd put them in my larder and cover them with
    soft brown earth.
    Oh dear, what shall we do . . .

If I were a woodpecker, you might see
Me flying to and from some hollow old tree
I'd hide some nuts in a crack in the bark,
Then I'd come back to get them when the days were cold
    and dark.

would-n't mind the rain. I'd search a - round on the

wood - land floor, And I'd stuff my face un - til I

could-n't eat a - no-ther bit___ more.

David Moses

Activities

Winter food stores – draw a chart like the one below adding to the animals given here. Add humans at the end and compare their shopping list, shops and storage places with those of the others.

ANIMAL.	SHOPPING LIST.	SHOPS.	LARDER
Hamster.	Nuts. Seeds. Grains.	Woodland floor.	In tummy or buried under leaves.
Bee.	Honey Pollen + nectar	Flowers.	Cells made of wax.
Marmot.	Grass Roots.	Meadows and prairies.	Cut and store in special burrows.
Beaver.	Twigs Bark	Forests.	Lodge built of logs and mud.
Nuthatch.	Acorns. Beechnuts. Chestnuts.	Woods.	Cracks in bark.

Accompaniment ideas

Link and chorus – see how cold and windy they can be made to sound. The part for recorder sounds like the wind – make it strong and gusty. What other sounds might add to the effect? – dry rustling leaves tossed up by the wind (maracas), the crack of dead wood (claves), shivering skin (shaken tambourine), more wind sounds (blow over the tops of pen-lids, or run a finger round the damp rim of a wine glass). Bring the sounds in at random rather than in regular rhythm.

Verse – the wind still whistles, but here the animals are bustling busily to find food for the winter, keeping warm while they work. Make the verse bustle along too. You could pick out some rhythms from the melody to play on percussion, using different instruments for the different animals, e.g. hamster:

Tambourine tapped lightly

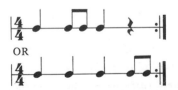

Forest rustler – tie a length of strong string across a room above head height. Thread onto short lengths of string collections of pasta shapes, beads, buttons, milk bottle tops, dried leaves, twigs, tinfoil, etc. Hang them from the horizontal string, which can be tapped or shaken to make it rustle.

Flying high, flying free

The red sun is sinking, the sky is on fire,
The swallows line up on the telegraph wire,
I think they've decided it's time to be gone,
For the days now are shrinking, the summer's moved on.
    Swallow, oh swallow, I wish I could follow you
    Over the deserts, the mountains, the sea,
    South to the colour and sunshine of Africa,
    Flying high, flying free.

Oh swallow, I don't understand how you know
How far you'll be flying and which way to go,
Resting at night time and flying by day,
With no map or compass to show you the way.
And I wish you could stay here the whole winter through,
Just as the robins and chaffinches do,
But I know that you can't for when frost grips the year,
The insects you feed on will all disappear.
    Swallow, oh swallow, I wish I could follow you ...

Butterfly, dragonfly, salmon and seal,
Whale and reindeer and cuckoo and eel,
All of you doing the migration dance,
And I'd do it, too, if they gave me the chance.
Clock on the mantelpiece, clock on the wall,
Clock in the kitchen and clock in the hall,
Tocking and ticking me off when I'm late,
But no clock to tell me it's time to migrate.
    Swallow, oh swallow, I wish I could follow you ...

I'll miss your forked tails as you sweep through the air
Your nests will be empty that you made with such care,
But I know you'll return as you have done before,
Your nests will be filled with your young ones once more.
So when Winter departs with his mantle of snow
And the plum tree's in flower and the days start to grow,
When the summer sun rises and the sky is on fire
I'll see you again on this telegraph wire.
    Swallow, oh swallow, I wish I could follow you ...

Chorus

Swal - low, oh swal-low, I wish I could fol - low you O - ver the de - serts, the moun-tains, the sea, South to the co - lour and sun - shine of A - fri - ca, Fly - ing high, fly - ing free.

Leon Rosselson

Accompaniment ideas

Tuned percussion – play the chords below throughout the song, changing where the guitar chords change.

The part for descant recorder, which mimics the swooping flight of the swallows, needs to be practised before fitting it in with the melody.

Winter on the farm

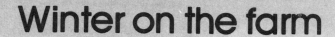

Winter on the farm, it's cold and wet,
Let's feed the animals, let's feed the animals,
There's mud on the ground, put your boots on your feet.
The sheep want some food to eat.
So we'll tramp, tramp, tramp,
Through the mud, mud, mud.
Tramp, tramp, tramp through the mud.
So we'll tramp, tramp, tramp,
Through the mud, mud, mud.
Tramp, tramp, tramp through the mud.

Winter on the farm, it's cold and wet,
Let's bring the cattle in, let's bring the cattle in,
There's snow in the fields, wrap your coat up tight,
The cows are coming home for the night.
So we'll trudge, trudge, trudge,
Through the snow, snow, snow . . .

Winter on the farm, it's cold and wet,
Let's lock the chickens up, let's lock the chickens up,
There's ice on the path, wrap your scarf round your head,
And we'll close up the chicken shed.
So we'll slide, slide, slide,
On the ice, ice, ice . . .

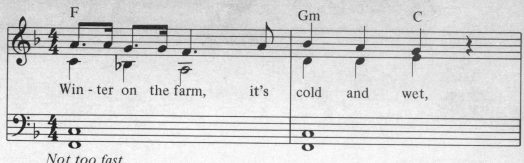

Not too fast

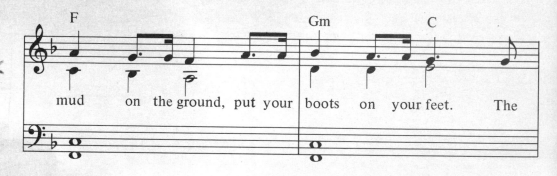

tramp, tramp, tramp, Through the mud, mud, mud.

Tramp, tramp, tramp through the mud. So we'll

tramp, tramp, tramp, Through the mud, mud, mud,

Tramp, tramp, tramp through the mud.

Harriet Powell

Accompaniment ideas
Tuned percussion

Verse x 8 *Chorus* x 2

Verse
Triangle

Tambourine (tapped very softly)
bars 3–4

x 2

(let's feed the a - ni - mals)

bars 7–8

Chorus
Bass drum

x 2

Alternative guitar chords
Capo at third fret

D	Em A	Em A₇	D A₇
D	Em A	A	D
G	D	A	D
G	D	A	D

59

One cold and frosty morning

One cold and frosty morning,
Just as the sun did rise,
The possum roared, the raccoon howled,
'Cause he began to freeze,
He drew himself up in a knot,
With his knees up to his chin,
And everything had to clear the track
When he stretched out again.

    The spring has come, you lazybones,
    Don't go to sleep again.
    The spring has come, you lazybones,
    Don't go to sleep again.

Welcome in the spring with the raccoon waking from hibernation. Pretend to sleep, then wake up and howl. Curl up in a knot, then on "spring", leap up stretching arms and legs wide.

Accompaniment ideas
The second part for voice or melody instrument may be played on piano (small notes in the bass stave of the piano accompaniment) either by one or two people. The symbols refer to:

△ triangle trill

✳ cymbal – one hard tap with a soft beater

drum roll on 'roared'

clappers on 'howled'

scraper on 'freeze'

swanee whistle – one long downward slide to 'chin' then up to 'again'.

Brown bear's snoring

Traditional Swedish

Brown bear's snor-ing, brown bear's snor-ing, In his win-ter sleep,

Brown bear's snor-ing, brown bear's snor-ing, In his win-ter sleep, But

snow and ice are mel - ting, I - ci - cles are drop-ping

Brown bear's ears are lis-tening and his eyes be-gin to peep.

The clear the track When he stretched out a — gain. The

spring spring has come, you la - zy - bones, Don't

1. has come. The come.

2. go to sleep a-gain. The gain.

Traditional American: collected by Mary McDaniel Parker

One child is chosen to be the brown bear, and curls up in the centre of a ring formed by the other children. They are the woodchucks, lemmings, squirrels, birds and insects which share the brown bear's home in the northern coniferous forests. As the song is sung and repeated, the little animals and birds move round the bear collecting food and getting closer to him. Gradually, the brown bear uncurls himself from sleep, yawns, stretches and may at any moment leap up to give chase. He must run on all fours, or on hands and knees, moving his right limbs together then his left. Brown bears are quite slow so the other animals have a good chance of escape – unless they push their luck too far.

Rainforests lie close to the Equator, within the tropics where annual rainfall is 50–100 inches (in Europe, annual rainfall is 20–30 inches), and temperatures are high all year with little seasonal variation. Nowhere is there a richer profusion of life than in these tropical hothouses – they contain half the species of plants and animals on Earth.

A rainforest is like a giant three-storey building, in which most of the occupants live on the top floor. About 100ft above the ground in the bright sunlight and rain, the crowns of the rainforest trees form a dense canopy of leaves, fruits and flowers, providing food and shelter to birds, insects, monkeys, flying squirrels, leopards, sloths, frogs, lizards and snakes. Lower down, the light dims rapidly. About 50 feet above the ground another sub-canopy is formed by the tops of smaller trees. Way down on the groundfloor, the air is stagnant, hot and steamy and very little light reaches it. But among the debris of leaves and fruits, which fall from above, the forest is sustained and recycled. Fungi, bacteria, ants and termites quickly break the material down and release the nutrients for the roots of the trees. Only about 1% of the goodness escapes in the rain.

The rainforests are disappearing at the rate of approximately 40 acres per minute and at this rate will be gone within 50–60 years. The trees are being cut for fuelwood, industrial wood, and to clear space for farming, cattle grazing, towns and roads. Tragically the soil is too poor to sustain more than one or two years of cultivation. As soon as it is overgrazed or farmed, more forest has to be cleared to replace it. The end result of unmanaged clearance is desertification. Countless species of animals and plants, many unknown to science, will disappear along with the rainforests and huge climatic changes may disrupt life all round the world. A South American legend tells that the trees hold up the sky – if they are cut down there will be catastrophe.

Life in the rainforest

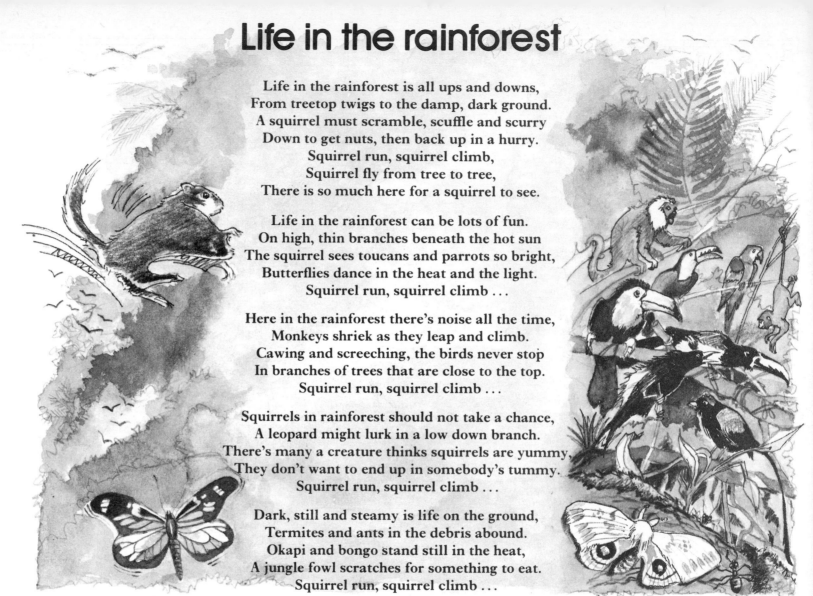

Life in the rainforest is all ups and downs,
From treetop twigs to the damp, dark ground.
A squirrel must scramble, scuffle and scurry
Down to get nuts, then back up in a hurry.
Squirrel run, squirrel climb,
Squirrel fly from tree to tree,
There is so much here for a squirrel to see.

Life in the rainforest can be lots of fun.
On high, thin branches beneath the hot sun
The squirrel sees toucans and parrots so bright,
Butterflies dance in the heat and the light.
Squirrel run, squirrel climb …

Here in the rainforest there's noise all the time,
Monkeys shriek as they leap and climb.
Cawing and screeching, the birds never stop
In branches of trees that are close to the top.
Squirrel run, squirrel climb …

Squirrels in rainforest should not take a chance,
A leopard might lurk in a low down branch.
There's many a creature thinks squirrels are yummy,
They don't want to end up in somebody's tummy.
Squirrel run, squirrel climb …

Dark, still and steamy is life on the ground,
Termites and ants in the debris abound.
Okapi and bongo stand still in the heat,
A jungle fowl scratches for something to eat.
Squirrel run, squirrel climb …

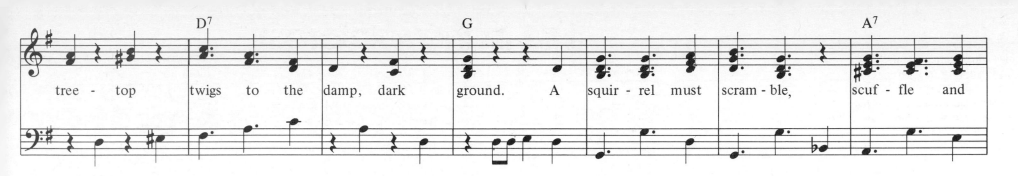

tree - top twigs to the damp, dark ground. A squir - rel must scram - ble, scuf - fle and

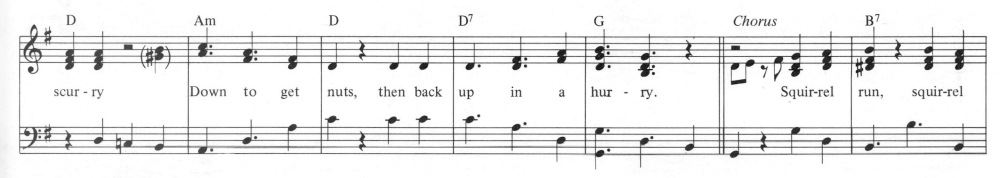

scur - ry Down to get nuts, then back up in a hur - ry. Squir-rel run, squir-rel

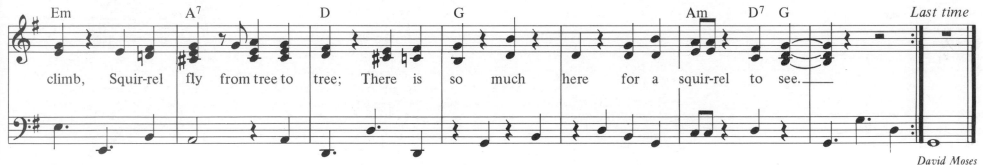

climb, Squir-rel fly from tree to tree; There is so much here for a squir-rel to see.

David Moses

Activities

Rainforest Support Group – discuss what action individuals or groups can take to help save the rainforests (see page 78). Design posters on the theme – *Save the Rainforests*. Write a leaflet to inform people about what is happening. Put together a rainforest display – a mini-exhibition: show where the forests are located on a map of the world, make graphs indicating the rate of destruction, display photographs and drawings of animals and plants, list the reasons for the forest clearances along with photographs before and after, describe the long-term consequences for human and animal life, list alternatives which could save the forests – careful management of tree felling, growing timber in plantations, establishing National Parks, providing alternative land for farmers, lessening the demand for meat, harvesting other products which can be extracted without causing damage, e.g. medicinal drugs.

First hand accounts – tell the story of the disappearing rainforests in the words of a landless farmer, a native Indian, a government official, and a clouded leopard.

Accompaniment ideas

Listen to a recording of rainforest sounds and think of ways of imitating them in the first, second and third verse (scrapers, recorders, maracas, a flexitone, etc.). During the fourth and fifth verses the sounds can become distant, and the singing hushed and a little slower.

When the melody is very familiar, improvise round the basic rhythm on bongos, e.g.

Basic rhythm

Variations

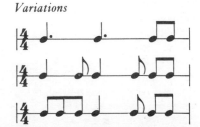

Ballad of the boll weevil

Monoculture – the farming of just one crop, such as wheat, tobacco or cotton – can bring high financial return, but problems as well. When large areas are devoted to one crop, the food plants which sustain a rich web of life are removed, encouraging large quantities of particular species, unmolested by natural predators, to concentrate and become pests. Just this occurred in the 1890s when the tiny boll weevil attacked the cotton fields of the American South, devastating entire crops and driving thousands of people off the land.

Diversifying and allowing natural pest control to rule can avoid this, but chemical fertilisers and pesticides have been used increasingly during this century to improve crop yields and keep pests at bay. It is a difficult process to reverse, as it can take years for soil to regain its natural fertility, and for food webs to recover, during which time the land is uncommercial.

Accompaniment ideas
This is a fast-moving song which needs a light accompaniment to keep up the momentum.

Chorus
Try playing the rhythm and notes below on 1. maracas and chimes, and 2. woodblock and xylophone.

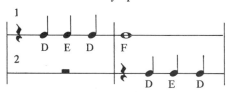

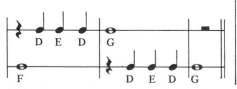

Well, the first time I saw the boll
    weevil,
He was standin' on the square.
The next time I saw the boll weevil,
He had his whole durn family there,
    They were lookin' for a home,
    They were lookin' for a home.

The farmer took the boll weevil,
And put him in a cake of ice,
The weevil said to the farmer,
Well, that's mighty cool and nice.
    This'll be my home …

The farmer took the boll weevil,
And he put him in the hot sand,
The weevil said, phew this is hot,
But I'll stand it like a man,
    Cos I need a home …

The next time I saw the boll weevil,
He was runnin' a spinnin' wheel,
The last time a saw the boll weevil,
He was ridin' in an automobile,
    Just enjoying his home …

Well the merchant got half the cotton,
The boll weevil got the rest,
Didn't leave that farmer's wife
But one old cotton dress,
    And it was full of holes …

Now, if anybody should ask you
Who it was that sang this song,
Tell them it was a poor farmer
Just been here and gone,
    And he's lookin' for a home …

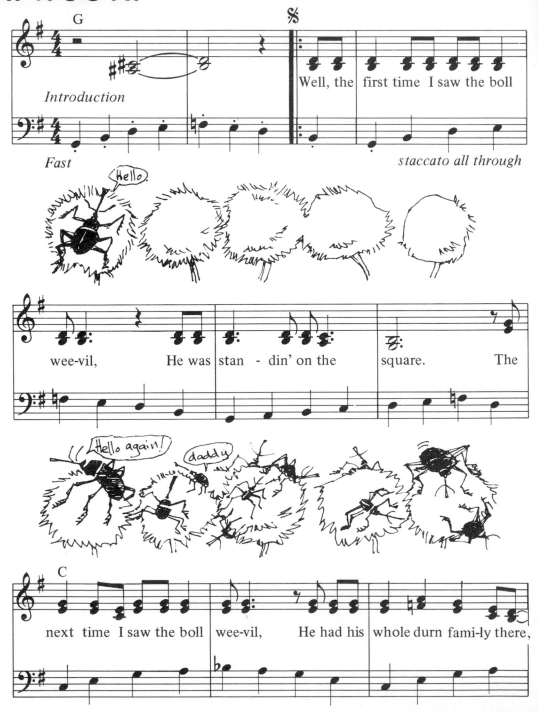

Webbing

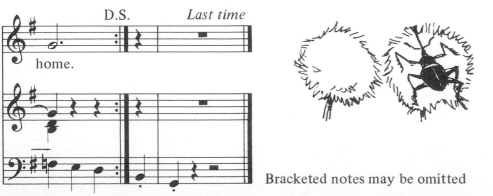

Bracketed notes may be omitted

The children form a circle, with the leader or teacher standing inside the circle near the edge with a ball of string. The leader asks:

Who can name a plant that grows in this area?

The answer may be dandelion in which case one person is chosen to be the dandelion and holds the end of the ball of string. Next the leader asks:

Is there an animal living around here that might eat this dandelion?

Rabbit may be the answer, and the string is passed to the person across the ring from the dandelion, connecting the two together. Next:

Who needs to eat this rabbit?

Continue connecting the children with string as their relationships to the rest of the group emerge. Bring in new elements and considerations, homes, soil, water, and so on, until the entire circle is strung together in a symbol of the web of life. You have created your own ecosystem.

To demonstrate how each individual is important to the whole community, take away one member of the web – perhaps a fire or a farmer kills a tree. When the tree falls, it tugs on the strings it holds; anyone who feels a tug is in some way affected by the death of the tree. Now everyone who felt a tug, *gives* a tug. Eventually every individual is affected by the destruction of the tree.

Butterfly flutterby

Butterfly, flutterby, please take care in the air,
There are birds on the wing, who will eat you, you tasty thing.
For your life is so short, if you're caught you'll be nought,
Butterfly, flutter by, butterfly.

Find a mate in the sun, lay your eggs safely now
On a leaf, underneath, that the caterpillars like to eat.
For your life is so short, if you're caught, you'll be nought,
Little egg, hatch out now – caterpillar.

Eat your way through the leaf, then you'll grow and you'll grow,
Then you'll change, you'll feel strange, weave a thread for a bed.
For your life is so short, if you're caught you'll be nought,
Caterpillar, go to sleep – chrysalis.

Rest a while, time to smile, you must wait for the spring,
When the sun and the warmth are for those on the wing.
For your life is so short, if you're caught you'll be nought,
Chrysalis, nearly there – butterfly.

Break your shell, stretch your wings, now go free in the air,
Please take care, do beware of the dangers everywhere.
For your life is so short, if you're caught you'll be nought –
Butterfly, tortoiseshell, painted lady, meadow brown,
Swallowtail, peacock blue, of every hue.

Gentle and not too fast

F   Bb   C7

— fly,   flut-ter —by,   but-ter —fly._____

slow down a little

⊕ *Coda*

F   Bb   F   Bb

— fly,   tor-toise -shell,   pain-ted   la-dy,   mea-dow   brown,   swal-low-

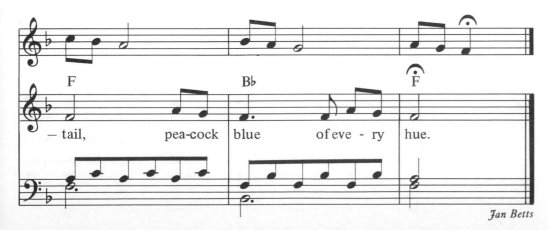

F   Bb   F

— tail,   pea-cock   blue   of eve - ry   hue.

Jan Betts

At every stage in their lifecycle, butterflies depend on the quality of their habitat for survival. When she is ready to lay her eggs, the female seeks out the right kind of plant to nourish the caterpillars when they emerge. Eggs may need to lie undisturbed for anything from six days to eight months. Having grown to its full size, the caterpillar is ready to pupate – another period when peace is required. As soon as the new butterfly breaks out of its pupa and dries its wings, it sets off in search of nectar to feed on and a mate, so that the whole process may begin again. Destruction and downgrading of habitat are the butterfly's worst enemies.

Activities

Butterfly gardening – gardens can provide a small protected nature reserve for butterflies, moths and other wild creatures whose habitat is shrinking. Find out how to provide the best quality habitat for different species of butterfly (perhaps those native to your area), then design a garden layout likely to attract them. This can be done as a class project, or each child could design their own individual garden for a different species of butterfly. Allow free choice in the size, shape and terrain of their garden design (provided it is suited to the chosen butterfly), then ask them to draw and paint an aerial plan showing the situation of the varieties of flowers, plants and trees. Different species will have different requirements, e.g. a hibernating butterfly like the small tortoiseshell will need a plentiful supply of nectar in early spring when it wakes. Good plants would be wallflowers, alyssum, aubretia and arabis. The tortoiseshell would then very much appreciate a bed of nettles, in which to lay eggs, and as food for her caterpillars.

Movement and dance – make up a butterfly dance to accompany the song. Take one step per bar, making wide, sweeping gestures with the arms, turning, dipping, hovering and fluttering.

Butterfly masks and face painting – look at photographs of butterflies, observing the wing shapes, and patterns. Cut butterfly-shaped masks out of card, or, in pairs, paint a butterfly on each other's face. Use your masks and painted faces for the dance.

Alternative guitar chords
Capo at third fret

```
||: D    |Fm  |G    |A7  :|| × 3
|  D    |G   |A7   |A7   ||
Coda
|  D    |G   |D    |D    |
|  G    |D   |G    |D    ||
```

Do you know the fox?

Do you know the fox with her coat so red?
She was born in a box, on a farm she was bred.
With her tail drooping down and a price on her head,
She is sad as a bird in a cage is –
Sad as a bird in a cage.

Do you know the trader? He puts profit first,
And the pockets of his coat hold a fat money purse
That he filled to the brim selling foxes furs.
He is greedy as a desert for a rainstorm –
Greedy as a desert for the rain.

Do you know the lady with her coat so rare?
It was lined with sorrow and stitched with care.
Her beauty is as deep as the skins that she wears
And her heart is as cold as a stone is –
Her heart is as cold as a stone.

Do you know the fox with her coat so red?
With her white-tipped tail and her long-muzzled head,
The heather is her cover and the earth is her bed,
She is free as a breeze in the willows –
Free as a breeze in the tree.

She is sad as a bird in a cage is

Sad as a bird in a cage.

Coda

Sandra Kerr

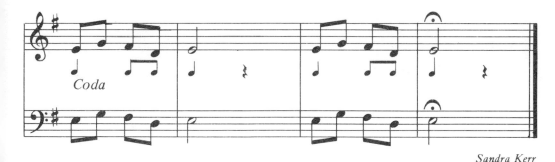

TUNED PERCUSSION (e.g. alto metallophone)   X 3

Accompaniment

Snare drum (or tapped shaker) – play the rhythm written in small notes above the bass stave, or the rhythm of the piano accompaniment, to give the effect of a rather menacing tattoo:

Play very softly, building up a crescendo through the first three verses then letting the drum fall silent in the last verse, where the rhythm becomes the running of the fox, wild and free.

Tuned percussion part – this works well on alto metallophone and soft beaters.

Look at the verses to see if there are any possibilities for word painting, e.g. tap the edge of a tambourine in the line 'and the pockets of his coat hold a fat money purse'; tap four times on a triangle in 'her *beauty* is as *deep* as the *skins* that she *wears*'. Think how to treat the words *cage*, *desert* and *stone*.

What sounds might give an impression of the fox's freedom in the last verse. It might be sung unaccompanied or with only a hint of the breeze rustling the willows and heather (maracas, cymbal rubbed with wire brush – play randomly).

Choose a melody instrument to play the introduction and coda.

In January 1981, a survey of Tokyo department stores revealed the following endangered spotted-cat coats for sale at prices ranging between £20,000 and £80,000: clouded leopard, tiger, snow leopard, ocelot, African leopard, Asian leopard.

These species and many others are protected by law and it is illegal to kill them or sell their furs in all countries bound by the 1973 Convention on International Trade in Endangered Species of Wild Fauna and Flora (CITES). But though the very rare species are increasingly difficult to trade in, laws give little or no protection to other, more common species, which continue to be trapped in the wild, or bred specially on farms for the fur trade. Trapping in the wild can be a brutal affair – the steel jaw leghold trap (like a gin trap) is widely used in North America. Farming animals for their fur takes some of the pressure off those in the wild, but it encourages

demand for real fur coats. Farming may seem more humane to us, but may not seem so to the untamed instincts of creatures such as the mink or fox.

Activities

Fur trade display. Make a collection of adverts for fur coats from magazines and newspapers and use them in a display of photographs or drawings of the original owners. Find out how many animals it takes to make a fur coat, and whether they are trapped or farmed. Make another display of fur alternatives using real materials if possible – man-made cloths, printed fabrics, wool, fur fabric.

Discussion – why do people use fur coats, who wears them, who is responsible for maintaining the fur trade, whose livelihoods are at stake, and what alternatives are there for them should the trade be outlawed completely; if it is not, what would the children consider a legitimate use of fur?

Rhino on the run

Sunrise over the Serengeti,
Creatures stir and begin their day.
One appears and the trees all tremble,
It's a young rhinoceros out to play!

  There's a one-ton, two-horned giant in the sun;
  It's a three-toed, four-legged rhino on the run.
  For he's all too rare, so do take care
  To shoot him with a camera and never with a gun.

Feeding time in the broad savannah,
White rhinoceros wander free;
Roll in dusty bath, feast on tender grass,
Snooze at peace in shade of tree.
  There's a one-ton, two-horned . . .

Sunset over the Serengeti,
To the water the thirsty creep.
White rhinoceros take your fill
And wander off to cover, then go to sleep.
  There's a one-ton, two-horned . . .

TREBLE RECORDER

Moderate

Sun - rise o — ver the Se — ren — ge - ti,

Crea - tures stir and be - gin their day. One ap - pears and the

trees all trem-ble, It's a young rhi - no - ce - ros out to play!

70

Children of Elland C of E Junior School

The whale

The whale, the whale,
The citizen of the sea,
He has the right to live
And so does she.
In the ocean, in the wild,
She moves peaceful with her child,
Till the harpoon wounds her young,
And she hovers to protect it,
And she's done.

The whale, the whale,
The citizen of the sea,
He sings his sonic song
And so does she.
He finds his mating ground
Till the whaler tracks him down,
Every quarter hour, they say,
One great whale is done away,
Done away.

The humpback and the blue,
The bowhead and the right,
Every quarter hour
Day and night.
Ocean creatures large and small,
There was room enough for all,
Till there came the rule of man,
Now the gentle whale is dogmeat
In the can.

The whale, the whale,
Four millions used to be
Their rightful population
In the sea.
Few thousands now remain
And we harry them again,
As the whale goes, and the dolphin,
And the ocean, and the forest,
So will we.

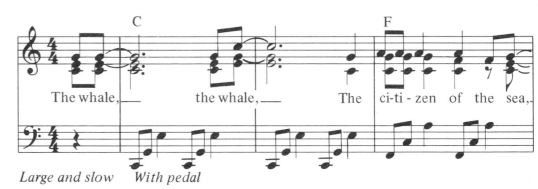

Large and slow   With pedal

Malvina Reynolds

child, Till the har - poon wounds her young, And she

ho-vers to pro-tect it, And she's done.

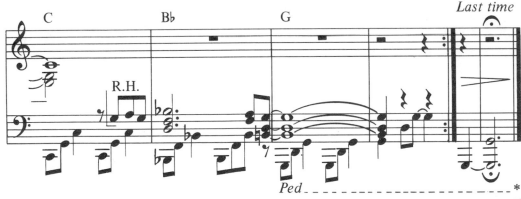

R.H.

Last time

Ped _ _ _ _ _ _ _ _ _ _ _ _ _ _ _ _ _ *

This song was written when whaling was still at its height. More than a decade later, after intense campaigning, whaling is very slowly being phased out.

Whales are highly intelligent mammals. They are very sociable, travelling in family groups and looking after their young for several years. They communicate by sound and have very individual voices and songs.

Once they swam in enormous numbers in all the oceans, but over centuries they have been pursued by whalers to the edge of extinction. First the whalers killed the right whales which fed in European coastal waters, and were very valuable, slow and easy to catch. By 1800 they had become commercially extinct in their traditional feeding grounds, so the whalers turned to the sperm and bowhead whales bringing them to commercial extinction. In 1865, the explosive harpoon was invented, and enabled whalers to catch faster whales like the humpback, fin, grey and the blue – the largest of all. Next, factory ships were built which could pursue the whales into their Antarctic feeding grounds, and the tolls rose still higher.

Today, whalers use helicopters, aeroplanes, ships, radar, ASDIC, and bombs which detonate inside the whale. The meat and oil is used for margarine, cosmetics, leather manufacture, lubricants and dogmeat. There are substitutes readily available for all these, so the continuation of whaling is unjustified.

The large whales like the blue, right, humpback, sperm and grey are all now protected, at least from legal whaling if not from pirate whalers. But in 1986 a complete ban on commercial whaling was circumvented by seven whaling nations (Japan, the USSR and Norway being the major ones) fixing their own quotas of sperm, minke, fin, brydes, pilot and sei whales.

Activities

Compile a report on the campaign to save the whales. When did it begin, how was it conducted, how successful has it been?

The song of the whale – scientists are still discovering more about the intelligence of whales through studying their complex 'songs' which they use to communicate with one another. It is thought that at one time these sounds could carry over a distance as great as between Antarctica and Alaska; nowadays the traffic noise of ships at sea causes too much interference. Listen to *The Songs of the Humpback Whale* recorded by Roger Payne (see page 78).

The dancing bear

My mother saw a dancing bear
By the schoolyard, a day in June.
The keeper stood with chain and bar
And whistle-pipe, and played a tune.

And bruin lifted up its head
And lifted up its dusty feet,
And all the children laughed to see
It caper in the summer heat.

They watched as for the Queen it died.
They watched it march. They watched
   it halt.
They heard the keeper as he cried,
'Now, roly-poly!' 'Somersault!'

And then, my mother said, there came
The keeper with a begging-cup,
The bear with burning coat of fur,
Shaming the laughter to a stop.

They paid a penny for the dance,
But what they saw was not the show;
Only, in bruin's aching eyes,
Far-distant forests, and the snow.

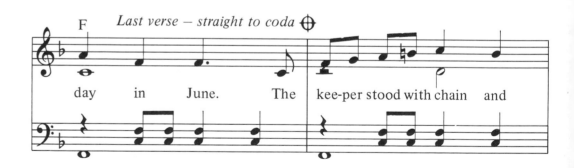

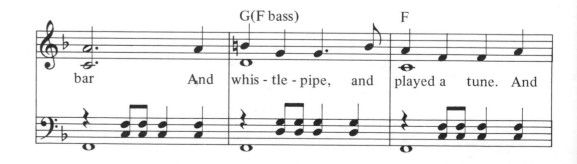

TUNED PERCUSSION

bru - in lif - ted up its head And lif - ted up its dus - ty feet, And all the chil - dren

Am⁷ (F bass)　　　　　　　B♭ (F bass)

laughed to see_ It ca - per in the sum — mer heat.

F　　　　　　　G(F bass)

⊕ *Coda*

On - ly, in bru - in's ach - ing eyes, Far - dis - tant fo - rests and the snow.___

F　　　　　　　G(F bass)　　　F

Charles Causley and Sandra Kerr

Accompaniment ideas
Tambour tapped very lightly with fingers all through except for the coda

Tambourine (tapped) or finger cymbals

Recorders – play the melody in verse 1, or as an interlude between verse 1 and 2.

My cat and I

My cat and I
Are friends,
That's why
We like to play together,
And be alone together.
When I do something bad
And Mum gets mad,
We like to play together
And be alone together;
And when I'm sent to bed
He curls up by my head,
And I can hear him purring
Through the pillow, softly purring.
And as I go to sleep
He lies down on my feet.
We fall asleep together,
My cat and I together.

My cat is white
With eyes that shine
At night.
We like to play together
And be alone together.
He drinks milk from a dish,
And smells a bit of fish.
We like to play together
And be alone together.
And when it starts to freeze
He curls up on my knees,
And I can feel him purring
On my lap, I feel him purring.
And when I read a book
He likes to have a look,
We read my book together,
My cat and I together.

David Moses

76

David Moses

Accompaniment ideas

The small notes in the melody line may be played by a melody instrument – e.g. glockenspiel or recorder – or voice singing 'meow'.

The symbols refer to

✳ tambourine, tapped once per asterisk

〰 scraper

Activities

Why have a pet? – discuss good and bad reasons for having pets, e.g. companionship, learning about animal behaviour, learning the responsibility for looking after them, as opposed to having them as status symbols or playthings.

Which pet? – divide into pairs. One person is the pet-shop assistant, the other is the customer. The customer thinks of an animal he or she wishes to have for a pet (allow free choice of any animal that may legally be imported into or bred in the country – see page 78 for information on trade in wild animals for pets). Having chosen, the customer gives a list of questions to the shop assistant to answer –

    How big will it grow?
    How much and what food will it eat?
    How much exercise will it need?
    What accommodation will it need?
    How often will it need cleaning out?
    How often will it breed?
    How long will it live?

Once the assistant has had time to answer these questions, he or she gives them to the customer who must then describe the ideal home for the animal, bearing in mind proper living quarters and special equipment, how the animal will be cared for during holidays, illness and old age, and estimating how much time and money will be required for proper care.

Finally the customer discusses the findings with the assistant and both decide whether the choice is a good one or not.

77

Odds and ends

Page 4 – answers to riddles: kangaroo, polar bear, squirrel, penguin.

Page 11 – names of young animals: kid – goat; fawn – deer; kit – weasel, otter; whelp – wolf; gosling – goose; cygnet – swan; squab – pigeon; eyas – hawk; larva – ant, bee; tadpole – frog; caterpillar – butterfly. Calves can grow into elephants, rhinos, hippos, antelopes, whales.

Page 17 – make a terrareum: in a plastic fish tank put a bottom layer of clay, followed by a layer of garden soil, then a thin layer of sand. Sprinkle some water onto the sand through a watering can rose so that it is evenly distributed, and so that the earth is damp without being soggy, then introduce a few worms to their temporary home. Keep the tank in a shady place and do not allow the soil to dry out. After a few days the bottom layer will have been taken to the top and the top to the bottom. Sprinkle a few semi-rotted leaves on top and see how they disappear, transported below ground by the worms, where they will be turned into a rich humus – the food of plants.

Page 23 – attracting and sustaining wildlife in towns. Many towns and cities have Urban Wildlife Groups. To find out if there is one in your area contact The Fairbrother Group (see address below).

Page 39 – the bird songs and calls in this sound story are based on recordings of blue tits made by Victor C. Lewis in *A Sound Guide to the British Tits*.

Page 63 – Rainforest Support Group: the organisation Earthlife (see address below), which works to save the world's rainforests, produces a *Schools Rainforest Resource Pack* which includes a booklet of information, wall charts, briefing sheets, reading and resource lists, and action-oriented information on setting up a local Rainforest Support Group as part of both classroom and extra-curricular work.

Books and recordings

GENERAL REFERENCE

The Amateur Naturalist, Gerald Durrell, Hamish Hamilton

Life on Earth: Reader's Digest Augmented and Enlarged Edition, David Attenborough, The Reader's Digest Association Ltd

The Living World of Animals, The Reader's Digest Association (out of print but still available in libraries.)

The Mitchell Beazley Atlas of World Wildlife

APPEARANCE – for teachers

The Guinness Book of Animal Facts and Feats, Wood, Guinness

A Field Guide in Colour to the Animal World, Octopus

APPEARANCE – for children

The Animal Book of Records, Tison and Taylor, Macdonald

Animals, Boorer, Macmillan

Zoo Animals in Colour, Kilpatrick, Octopus

How to Find Out About Animals, Barber and Eason, Studio Vista

Crafts

Animals to make, World Wildlife Fund, published by Scholastic Publications Ltd in association with WWF

The Complete Book of Paper Mask Making, Grater, Dover Publications

HABITAT – for teachers

See general reference books listed above.

HABITAT – for children

Life in the Wild, Oakley, Macmillan World Library

Life in the Water, Porter, Macmillan World Library

Private Lives of Animals series (Animals of Lake and Marsh, Animals of Oceans and Deep Seas, etc) published by F. Warne

MOVING ALONG – for teachers

Animal Locomotion, Gray, (World Naturalist series) Weidenfeld & Nicholson

MOVING ALONG – for children

Alive and Active, Stodart and Knight, Hodder & Stoughton

Animal Jumpers, Animal Runners, Animal Climbers, Animal Swimmers, Lilly, Walker Books

ANIMAL TALK – for teachers

Animal Language, Bright, BBC

The Oxford Companion to Animal Behaviour, ed. MacFarland, Oxford University Press

ANIMAL TALK – for children

Gobble Growl Grunt, Spier, World's Work

DEFENCES – for children

Animal Weapons, Animal Disguises, Animals That Live in Groups, Vevers, Bodley Head

How Animals Hide, McClung, National Geographic Society

Tricks Animals Play, Clarkson, National Geographic Society

ANIMALS IN WINTER – for children

Animal Homes and **Animals That Sleep in Winter,** Vevers, Bodley Head

ANIMALS AND US – for teachers

The Back Garden Wildlife Sanctuary Book, Wilson, Penguin Books

The Endangered Species Handbook, Nilsson, The Animal Welfare Institute, PO Box 3650, Washington DC 20007

The Gaia Atlas of Planet Management, Myers, Pan Books

Sharing Nature with Children, Joseph Bharat Cornell, Exley Publications in association with Inter-Action Inprint

The Use and Abuse of Animals, Richmond-Watson, (Debate Series) Macdonald

Working with Animals Jennings, Batsford

ANIMALS AND US – for children

Animals and Man, published by Purnell

Endangered Species Project, World Wildlife Fund–UK Education Department

How to Make a Wildlife Garden, Baines, Elm Tree Books

Sounds Natural – A World Wildlife Songbook, published by Boosey & Hawkes Music Publishers. Record/cassette available from the World Wildlife Fund–UK Education Department

Wildlife Action Book (projects, puzzles and games) World Wildlife Fund–UK Education Department

Yanomamo – A Musical Entertainment (cassette, booklet, and score) about Yanomami forest people and the ecology of the Amazonian rainforest, published by the World Wildlife Fund–UK Education Department

AUDIO/VISUAL RESOURCES

National Audio Visual Aids Library, The George Building, Normal College, Bangor, Gwynedd LL57 2PZ (Tel 0248 355155) produces a listing of audio-visual material for use in schools, colleges, and training centres, and also distributes the majority of items listed. The relevant volume is *Part 6(i) Palaeontology, Biology, Botany, Zoology*

BBC Records and Tapes – Sound Effects catalogue.

Sounds Natural (audio cassettes, slide sets and tape/slide packs including recordings of animals), catalogue from Ken Jackson, Upper End, Fulbrook, Oxford OX8 4BX

Acknowledgements

Songs of the Humpback Whale recorded by Dr Roger Payne, CRM Records

The Lion on the Path, African animal stories recorded by Hugh Tracey, available from Folktrack Cassettes, 16 Brunswick Square, Gloucester

Organisations

The voluntary and statutory environmental organisations which provide materials for use in schools and colleges are listed in:

Environment Education Enquiries, Conservation Trust

Directory for the Environment, Michael J. C. Barker, Routledge and Kegan Paul

This is a selection:

British Trust for Conservation Volunteers, 36 St Mary's Street, Wallingford, Oxon OX10 0EU

Council for Environmental Education, Reading University, London Road, Reading, Berkshire RG1 5AQ

The Fairbrother Group (urban wildlife groups), 11 Albert Street, Birmingham B4 7UA

Earthlife, 10 Belgrave Square, London SW1X 8PH

Friends of the Earth, 377 City Road, London EC1V 1NA

Royal Society for Nature Conservation, The Green, Nettleham, Lincoln LN2 2NR (Co-sponsors of WATCH, a national club for young people interested in the environment)

Royal Society for the Protection of Birds, The Lodge, Sandy, Bedfordshire SG19 2DL

World Wildlife Fund–UK, Education Department, Panda House, 11–13 Ockford Road, Godalming, Surrey GU7 1QU

The following copyright owners have kindly granted their permission for the inclusion of words, music, and games:

Sue Beer for 'The Lost Hippos'.

Elizabeth Bennett and Tom Stanier for the music and first verse of 'Who saw the footprints?'

Jan Betts for 'Urban hedgehog' and 'Butterfly flutterby'.

Campbell Connelly & Co, Ltd for 'Never Smile at a Crocodile', music by Frank Churchill, words by Jack Lawrence, copyright © 1952 by Walt Disney Music Company, USA. This arrangement © 1986 by Walt Disney Music Company used by A & C Black Publishers Ltd by kind permission of Campbell Connelly & Co Ltd, 78 Newman St, London W1P 3LA.

Chantelle Music Ltd for 'Follow my leader' by Jenyth Worsley.

Chappell Music Ltd and International Music Publications for 'Inchworm' by Frank Loesser, © 1951 Frank Loesser, Frank Music Corp (USA) and Anglo-Pic Music Co Ltd (UK).

Exley Publications Ltd for 'Noah's Ark', 'Bat and Moth', 'Webbing' and 'How many birds?' from *Sharing Nature With Children* by Joseph Bharat Cornell.

Folklore Productions Inc for 'Lots of worms' words and music by Patty Zeitlin, © 1973, Bullfrog Ballades (ASCAP).

Harvard University Press for 'One Cold and Frosty Morning' (*Old Jessie*) from *On the Trail of Negro Folk Songs* by Dorothy Scarborough, © 1925 by Harvard University Press and © 1953 by Mary McDaniel Parker. Reprinted by permission.

David Higham Associates Ltd for the words of 'The dancing bear' from *Figgie Hobbin* by Charles Causley, published by Macmillan.

Elizabeth Hogg for 'The Hopper', 'Old friends' and 'Question Mark?'

David Moses for 'Chicks grow into chickens' and 'My cat and I'.

Nonviolence and Children Committee, Philadelphia Yearly Meeting, 1515 Cherry Street, Philadelphia, PA 19102 for the game 'Elephants and Camels' from *A Manual on Nonviolence and Children*.

Harriet Powell for 'Farmer in the fog' and 'Winter on the farm'.

Cynthia Raza for 'Spotty song'.

Routledge and Kegan Paul for 'The Broomsquire's birdsong' from *The Chime Child* by Ruth Tongue.

Scholastic Publications Ltd for 'Wild and wary' by David Moses.

Schroder Music Company (ASCAP) for 'Says the Bee' by Malvina Reynolds, © copyright 1957 Schroder Music Co; 'You can't make a turtle come out' by Malvina Reynolds, © copyright 1963 Schroder Music Co; 'The whale' by Malvina Reynolds, © copyright 1974 Schroder Music Co. Used by permission. All rights reserved.

Westminster Music Ltd for 'Kangaroos like to hop', words and music by Leon Rosselson, © 1968 Westminster Music Ltd.

The World Wildlife Fund for 'Rhino on the Run'.

Particular thanks are due to the following who wrote material specially for inclusion in this book:

Jan Betts ('Urban hedgehog' and 'Butterfly flutterby').

Veronica Clark ('Sea dive' and 'Body language').

Sandra Kerr ('Hi, said the elephant', 'Do you know the fox?' and the music of 'The dancing bear').

Surya Kumari ('The yogi and the cobra').

David Moses ('Winter food stores' and 'Life in the rainforest').

Harriet Powell ('Which animal?', 'Birds are flying'and 'Hide!').

Leon Rosselson ('Free to roam' and 'Flying high, flying free').

Peter Stacey ('The blue tits and the cat' and, with Biddy Wells, 'Rondo zoo').

79

Index